# Muhammad

*These and other titles are included in The Importance Of biography series:*

# Muhammad

by Marilyn Tower Oliver

LUCENT
BOOKS®

THOMSON

™

GALE

San Diego • Detroit • New York • San Francisco • Cleveland • New Haven, Conn. • Waterville, Maine • London • Munich

THOMSON

GALE

To my grandmother, Ruby Barham

**LIBRARY OF CONGRESS CATALOGING-IN-PUBLICATION DATA**

Oliver, Marilyn Tower.
   Muhammad / by Marilyn Tower Oliver.
      p.  cm. — (The importance of)
Includes bibliographical references and index.
Summary: Profiles the life of Muhammad and his founding of the religion known as Islam.
   ISBN 1-59018-232-4
    1. Muhammad, Prophet, d. 632—Biography.   2. Muslims—Saudi Arabia—Biography.
[1. Muhammad, Prophet, d. 632.  2. Prophets.  3. Islam.]  I. Title.  II. Series.
BP75.O36 2003
   297.6'3—dc21
[B]
                                  2002011291

Printed in the United States of America

# Contents

# Foreword

THE IMPORTANCE OF biography series deals with individuals who have made a unique contribution to history. The editors of the series have deliberately chosen to cast a wide net and include people from all fields of endeavor. Individuals from politics, music, art, literature, philosophy, science, sports, and religion are all represented. In addition, the editors did not restrict the series to individuals whose accomplishments have helped change the course of history. Of necessity, this criterion would have eliminated many whose contribution was great, though limited. Charles Darwin, for example, was responsible for radically altering the scientific view of the natural history of the world. His achievements continue to impact the study of science today. Others, such as Chief Joseph of the Nez Percé, played a pivotal role in the history of their own people. While Joseph's influence does not extend much beyond the Nez Percé, his nonviolent resistance to white expansion and his continuing role in protecting his tribe and his homeland remain an inspiration to all.

These biographies are more than factual chronicles. Each volume attempts to emphasize an individual's contributions both in his or her own time and for posterity. For example, the voyages of Christopher Columbus opened the way to European colonization of the New World. Unquestionably, his encounter with the New World brought monumental changes to both Europe and the Americas in his day. Today, however, the broader impact of Columbus's voyages is being critically scrutinized. *Christopher Columbus,* as well as every biography in The Importance Of series, includes and evaluates the most recent scholarship available on each subject.

Each author includes a wide variety of primary and secondary source quotations to document and substantiate his or her work. All quotes are footnoted to show readers exactly how and where biographers derive their information, as well as provide stepping stones to further research. These quotations enliven the text by giving readers eyewitness views of the life and times of each individual covered in The Importance Of series.

Finally, each volume is enhanced by photographs, bibliographies, chronologies, and comprehensive indexes. For both the casual reader and the student engaged in research, The Importance Of biographies will be a fascinating adventure into the lives of people who have helped shape humanity's past and present, and who will continue to shape its future.

## Important Dates in the Life of Muhammad

**570**
Birth of Muhammad
at Mecca

**615**
Some Muslims
emigrate to
Abyssinia

**621**
First Pledge of
al'Aqabah

**610–613**
The first three years
of Muhammad's
ministry

**620**
First converts
from Yathrib
(Medina) come
to Mecca

**595**
Muhammad marries
Khadijah, a widow

570          595          620

**610**
Muhammad receives his first revelation

**613**
Muhammad begins to speak publicly

**616–619**
Muhammad and the Hashim clan
are boycotted by the Quraysh

**619**
Muhammad's night visit to Jerusalem
Deaths of Khadijah and Abu Talib

**622**
Second Pledge of al'Aqabah
The migration (*hijra*) to Yathrib
**June 18, 622** Muhammad escapes from Mecca
**June 28, 622** Muhammad arrives at Qoaba near Mecca

**624**
**March 15** Battle of Badr
**October** to **January 625** Break with Jewish tribes
Direction of prayer changed from Jerusalem to Mecca
Friday becomes the Muslim day of prayer

**628**
**March**—Treaty of
Hudabiyah

**630–631**
Muhammad receives
delegations from
Arabian tribes to
pay tribute

**627**
**April**—Extermination
of the Bani Qurayzah
Jews

625

630

635

**625**
**March** Battle of Uhud
**August–September** Siege
of the Nadir Jews and
their exile

**630**
**January**—The conquest
of Mecca
**February–March**—
Muslim siege of Taif

**623**
**January** to **October**
Muslims start raids
against Meccan
caravans and city of
Nakhlah

**632**
**March 9** The farewell
pilgrimage to Mecca
**May**—Muhammad
becomes ill
**June 8**—Death of
Muhammad

**629**
**February**—Muslims make lesser
pilgrimage to Mecca

# The Founder of Islam

Although he lived more than fourteen hundred years ago, the impact of the prophet Muhammad ibn Abd Allah, founder of Islam, on the direction of world history reaches across the centuries to touch people living in every corner of the world. Although the followers of Islam, Muslims, do not regard him as a saint, they honor him as the person through which Allah, the Arabic word for God, spoke to humankind to tell them that there was only one God and that they should practice good deeds as taught in their holy book, the Koran. They also revere him because of his remarkable life.

Today, the appeal of Islam is undeniable. The religion claims more than a billion followers in the Middle East, Asia, Europe, and North America, making it the second largest religious group in the world after Christianity. It is also the world's fastest growing religion. Although many people associate the religion with Arabs, the three countries with the largest communities of Muslims are in the Asian countries of Indonesia, Pakistan, and Bangladesh. Since the 1950s, large numbers of Muslims have also emigrated to Europe and America to study

and work. In many countries of Europe and North America they have become a significant and rapidly growing minority.

Five times a day these believers face Mecca, the holy city of their religion, and proclaim, *"La ilaha illa Allah . . . Muhammad rasul Allah."* "There is no god but Allah. Muhammad is the messenger of Allah." Who was the man who made such a difference in the lives of the many followers of Islam, and why has his life continued to affect so many people for more than thirteen hundred years? Although he had great spiritual insights, Muhammad was very involved in the world in which he lived. He was a good businessman, a loving husband and father, a skilled military strategist, and a politician.

## SOURCES OF INFORMATION ABOUT MUHAMMAD'S LIFE

Unfortunately, very little factual information exists about the years of Muhammad's life before he began to receive spiritual revelations at the age of forty, because there are no known written accounts dating from that time. There is also very sparse information about the first years when he began to gather converts in Mecca.

Much of what we know about Muhammad comes from the Koran, the holy book of Islam, which is made up of verses that were revealed to him during his lifetime. Although the Koran gives Muslims rules for daily living and is a guide for their spiritual practices, it also makes indirect references to events that took place during Muhammad's life. As Muhammad received the revelations, he told them to his followers, some of whom wrote them down. Others memorized them, as was the custom of the time. About twenty years after his death, these revelations were gathered into one collection by his followers. They were not arranged according to the order in which they were received by Muhammad, so they do not read as a historical narrative.

Another source of information comes from a collection of stories that began as oral reports about events that took place in Muhammad's life. As his importance as a leader emerged, his followers began to gather stories about events that had taken place earlier in his life. Told by his early friends and companions to later generations, these anecdotes became known as the *Hadith*, an Arabic word that means "reports." The *Hadith* relates incidents that took place during Muhammad's childhood, his military and political accomplishments, and his family and spiritual life. The stories circulated among the followers of Muhammad in both oral and written form.

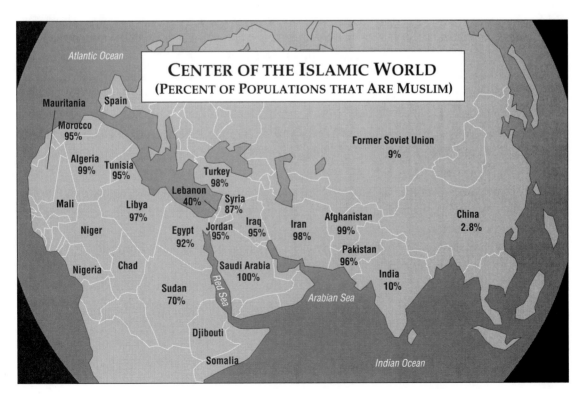

**CENTER OF THE ISLAMIC WORLD**
(PERCENT OF POPULATIONS THAT ARE MUSLIM)

Atlantic Ocean

Mauritania  Spain

Morocco
95%

Algeria   Tunisia
99%    95%

Turkey
98%

Former Soviet Union
9%

Lebanon
40%   Syria
87%

Mali    Libya
97%

China
2.8%

Niger    Egypt   Jordan   Iraq    Iran    Afghanistan
92%    95%    95%    98%    99%

Pakistan
96%

Nigeria   Chad    Saudi Arabia
100%

India
10%

Red Sea

Arabian Sea

Sudan
70%

Djibouti

Somalia

Indian Ocean

*By studying biographical verses in the Koran, a teacher helps a student interpret the life of Muhammad.*

As time passed and more people converted to Islam, many additional stories were added to the *Hadith*. Because Muhammad was loved and honored as a prophet, some of the stories were exaggerated narrations of actual events. Others described supernatural events that try to illustrate his remarkable qualities. By the eighth and ninth centuries, Muslim scholars became concerned that many of the stories that were circulating in the *Hadith* were inaccurate. To compile more accurate accounts, they took on the difficult task of determining which of the stories were most likely to be true. By this time the Muslim faith had spread to many countries far from Arabia, so the scholars had to travel to collect and verify the many different accounts about Muhammad's life. Their efforts led to the accounts that make up the *Hadith*, which today is studied in Islamic universities around the world.

In their works these early biographers attempted to make accurate historical reconstructions of the life of Muhammad.

They told where their information came from, including the sources for stories that had an oral source. Some of their accounts were unflattering. In some cases, they do not agree with one another. The stories of the *Hadith* that are found in the early biographies and the biographical verses in the Koran are what modern historians use to piece together the life of Muhammad. He has also been depicted in art over the centuries, although images of him often do not show his facial features because it is considered disrespectful in some Islamic countries.

During his lifetime, Muhammad succeeded in bringing the people of much of the Arabian peninsula together to worship one god, Allah. His mission, which at first was made up of a handful of followers, rapidly expanded to much of the Middle East and North Africa. Fifteen centuries later, the religion continues to make a political and cultural impact on the world.

# 1 The Beginning: Before the Revelations

Although during the first forty years of Muhammad's life, he was respected for his judgment and dependability, there were few signs of his future importance as a spiritual, political, and military figure. Scholars have few hard facts about these years, but through the early biographies they have been able to reconstruct some of the events of his childhood and adolescence.

## FAMILY AND BIRTH

It is believed that Muhammad was born in the city of Mecca on the Arabian peninsula around 570 B.C. This date was determined from accounts that say he was born in the Year of the Elephant, named for a battle in which the people of Mecca defended their city against a powerful Abyssinian army that outnumbered them. The Meccans were amazed by the sight of an armored elephant that accompanied the enemy troops.

Muhammad's father's family belonged to the Hashim clan or tribe, which was part of a larger tribal group called the Quraysh, the dominant tribe of Mecca. Al-

though the Hashim clan was not wealthy, it was well respected. His grandfather, Abdul Muttalib, was a respected civic leader and merchant who traded with the neighboring countries of Syria and Yemen. His family was made up of a number of wives from different tribes, ten sons, and six daughters. The historian Muhammad ibn Sa'd wrote that his sons were particularly good looking. "Among the Arabs there were no more prominent and stately men, none of more noble profile."[1]

Abdul Muttalib also had special privileges at the Ka'aba, the most important shrine in Mecca. Every year people from many parts of the Arabian peninsula made a pilgrimage called the *hajj* to worship at the cube-shaped, granite building, which was surrounded by 360 idols. The idols represented the many gods who were worshiped in the sixth- and seventh-century Arabian society. Although many Arabians believed that the Ka'aba had been originally dedicated to Allah, whom they considered to be the highest god, prior to Islam they also worshiped many lesser gods and goddesses. By the sixth and seventh centuries, Allah's authority as the primary god had declined and was replaced by these more popular deities. One of these was the god Hubal whose statue was the most prominent idol in the Ka'aba. The Ka'aba was the most important shrine in Arabia, but outside Mecca there were others such as those dedicated to the three daughters of Allah, fertility goddesses named Manat, al-Uzzah, and al-Lat. Some Arabs also worshiped spirits that lived in stones, trees, and springs.

At one side of the Ka'aba Abdul Muttalib had discovered a hidden spring called Zamzam, which the Arabs believed to be holy. Because of this discovery, Abdul Muttalib had the privilege of providing water from the spring and food to the pilgrims when they came to make the *hajj*.

Muhammad's father was a young man named Abd Allah or Abdullah, the youngest son of Abdul Muttalib, and supposedly his favorite. Muhammad's mother was a young Quraysh woman named Aminah. Like most marriages at the time, theirs was arranged. The young couple had been married only a few months when Abdullah left on a trading caravan that was headed to Syria. On the trip home he fell ill and stopped in the town of Yathrib, now known as Medina, to recover. Tragically, his illness was fatal, and he died leaving Aminah expecting a child. Because he died before he had accumulated much wealth, he left her with only a small inheritance consisting of five camels, a small flock of sheep and goats, and a female slave.

*Muhammad, in his mother Aminah's arms, is shown to his grandfather, Abdul Muttalib, for the first time.*

A short time later, when Aminah gave birth to a son, she sent the news to her father-in-law, Abdul Muttalib, who was responsible for naming the child. According to the legends surrounding Muhammad's birth, it took Abdul Muttalib seven days to come up with what was considered at the time an unusual name, Muhammad, which means "the Praised One." His full name was Muhammad ibn (son of) Abd Allah.

## AN EARLY CHILDHOOD IN THE DESERT

Although very little hard, factual information is known about

Muhammad's early life, most of his biographers believe that his mother followed the Quraysh custom of sending infants to live in the desert with nomadic Bedouin families for the first years of their lives. It was believed that the sparsely populated desert was a healthier environment in which to raise a young child than the crowded neighborhoods of Mecca.

Shortly after Muhammad's birth, a group of Bedouin women from the Bani Sa'd tribe came to Mecca to look for babies to nurse. Because this tribe had a good reputation for rearing young children, their services were in demand. In return for their services, the nomadic families often formed alliances with powerful families from the town. A foster mother hoped that the child she nursed would consider her as his second mother. She might also receive money and other favors from the child's father. However, when Aminah told them that Muhammad's father was dead, most refused to accept him as a foster child. It was felt that a single mother could not provide enough advantages to the Bedouin family that would nurture the child through his early years.

Eventually, all the women of the Bani Sa'd tribe found babies to nurse except for one very poor woman named Halimah. Because this had been a year of famine, she suffered from malnutrition and had barely enough milk to nurse her own baby son. Reluctant to return to the desert without a foster baby, she eventually agreed to take Muhammad back with her to nurse.

Muhammad's biographers differ as to how long he stayed with Halimah's fam-

ily. Some say that he remained with his Bedouin family until he was about six years of age. Others say he was brought back to his mother in Mecca when he was between two and three. He seems to have had a warm feeling toward his foster family, because years later he welcomed Halimah into his home when she came to visit, and when a drought had reduced her herds, he gave her a gift of forty sheep and a camel.

## A YOUNG ORPHAN

After Muhammad rejoined his mother in Mecca, he enjoyed the warmth of his grandfather's large extended family where there were many aunts and uncles to help nurture him. His uncles, 'Abbas and Hamzah, were about the same age as Muhammad. He formed a bond with Hamzah that lasted through adulthood. There were also many cousins for him to play with.

In 576, when Muhammad was six, Aminah decided to take him on a trip to the city of Yathrib, where she had relatives. Accompanied by their female slave, they joined a northbound caravan. Muhammad seemed to enjoy his visit to Yathrib, where he met another group of relatives and enjoyed new experiences. Years later he told followers that he had learned to swim in a pool at one relative's home. His young relatives also taught him how to fly a kite.

Later that year, Muhammad, Aminah, and the slave joined a caravan for the return trip to Mecca. They had barely started on the journey when Aminah be-

## Mecca

In the sixth century, Mecca was a commercial and religious center on the Arabian peninsula. Located less than sixty miles from the Red Sea, halfway between the seaport of Aden in Yemen and the town of Gaza on the Mediterranean, it was a crossroads between east and west. The city is surrounded by arid desert and low, barren hills where little grows. In Muhammad's time Mecca was a trading hub. Every winter camel caravans would go to Aden to obtain spices, ivory, silks, jewels, and other exotic goods brought by ship from India. In the summer, caravans would depart from Mecca to take the merchandise to Ethiopia, and in the winter they would set off for Syria. The caravans

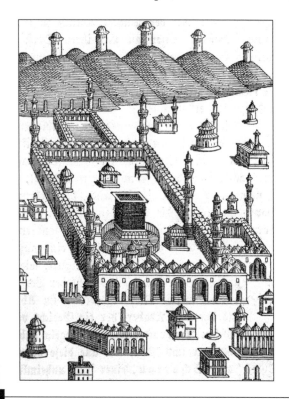

would return to Mecca with grain, olive oil, wine, fabrics, and sometimes weapons. Many of the caravans were very large, consisting of two thousand to twenty-five hundred camels and several hundred men who worked as guards, guides, and camel drivers. If the caravan could make its trip safely without encountering robbers, the wealthy investors made a great profit. The caravans also made the Meccans familiar with distant lands of the Byzantine and the Persian empires. Today, Muslims consider Mecca to be their holiest city, and each Muslim desires to make a pilgrimage there at least once in his or her lifetime.

*A fifteenth-century illustration of Mecca depicts the shrine Ka'aba in the center of the city.*

came very ill, forcing them to leave the caravan. A few days later, she died leaving the young boy orphaned. Shortly after his mother's burial, Muhammad and the slave girl were able to join a group of travelers back to Mecca. At first he was cared

for by the slave, but soon, his grandfather Abdul Muttalib, who was then eighty years old, took him into his household where he was treated well.

The child often accompanied his grandfather to the Ka'aba and to the Assembly, where the leaders of the town met to discuss the issues of the day. Two years later, in 578, Muhammad's life was again disrupted when his loving grandfather died. Before he died, however, Abdul Muttalib asked one of Muhammad's uncles, Abu Talib, to take the young child into his family. Precise historical facts about Muhammad's life in Abu Talib's household are scarce, and those that exist come largely from Ibn Ishaq's book, *The Life of the Prophet,* which was written in the eighth century.

Although Abu Talib was respected in Mecca as a leader of the Hashim tribe, he was not wealthy. He earned his living by pasturing sheep and goats and by conducting trading caravans to Syria and other Middle Eastern countries. Although he had four children of his own to support, he fully accepted his orphaned nephew into his family, where Muhammad enjoyed the friendship of Abu Talib's sons who were close to him in age. Like other young Arab boys, Muhammad also had chores. Many years later, when he saw people carrying fruit from the arak tree, a thorny bush used to feed camels and other animals, Muhammad spoke of one of his childhood responsibilities. "It was those I gathered when I used to lead the sheep out to graze,"[2] he said.

In spite of the affection of Abu Talib's family, it appears that Muhammad's unstable childhood affected his personality. The British historian Sir John Glubb writes, "Muhammad seems to have been a serious child. The insecurity of his infancy may have made him quiet and thoughtful beyond his years."[3]

## MUHAMMAD'S EDUCATION

Very little is known about Muhammad's education and childhood in Abu Talib's family. Scholars disagree on whether or not he was taught to read or write, because later in his life he relied upon his followers to write down the revelations he received in order to preserve them. Formal schools were nonexistent in seventh-century Mecca. It is known that his uncle, Abu Talib, made sure that his nephew and sons received some education in the use of weaponry and in self-defense, like archery, wrestling, and sword fighting. Muhammad was competent at these sports, but his excellent vision helped him develop great skill as an archer. It was said that his eyesight was so keen that he could count at least twelve of the stars of the constellation of the Pleiades.

It is likely that most of his education was the hands-on training that he received while accompanying his uncles on trading journeys with their caravans. The caravans were an important part of Meccan life because they brought prosperity to the town. There were two larger caravans each year and also a number of smaller ones. The large caravans consisted of several thousand camels and hundreds of men, horses, and donkeys, which were protected by armed guards. The caravans transported goods from as far away as India and China, taking them eastward for sale in Egypt and Syria. Most of the trips Muhammad made were to Syria. They gave him exposure to different customs, cultures, and religions such as Christianity and Judaism. These two

## TRIBAL LIFE

In the sixth century and before, Arabia did not have a central government. Most of the people belonged to clans or tribes that were led by a leader called a *shayk*. Tribal affiliations offered them protection and an identity and gave help to the weak and the needy. In return, people were expected to have loyalty to their tribe, which afforded them safety. If the tribe or anyone in it were attacked, it would be necessary to retaliate by fighting back. Smaller clans were clustered into larger tribal units such as the Quraysh, the dominant tribe of Mecca. While the inhabitants of Mecca could earn a living from trading with other countries, most Arabians were nomads who moved from place to place in search of green oases where their herds could graze.

In the book *Mohammedanism*, D.S. Margoliouth writes:

> The society of Arabia was founded on the theory of the joint responsibility of the tribe, especially for bloodshed; and it would seem that the death of a tribesman at the hands of a member of another tribe led to a long and complicated series of battles and assassinations, the purpose of which was not to gain any decisive results, such as the acquisition of territory or the subjugation of a community, but retaliation with interest. When the warring communities got tired or exhausted, the numbers of slain on either side were counted up, and any surplus paid for.

religions have a strong belief in monotheism, the existence of one god, which may have influenced Muhammad's later beliefs.

During his adolescence Muhammad also began to take part in the religious and political activities of Mecca. It is believed that he belonged to a society or brotherhood called *hums*, which practiced special rituals at Meccan religious ceremonies.

At this time the peace of Mecca was disturbed by periodic disputes between Muhammad's tribe, the Quraysh, and neighboring tribes. The disputes resulted in only five-day-long battles. Muhammad's uncles took him to one of the first battles, but said he was too young to fight.

To help out, he was allowed to pick up the enemy arrows that fell on the ground and hand them to his uncles who reused them. It is reported that at a second battle he was permitted to fight and that he was praised for his skill as an archer.

Another dispute led the Quraysh to call for a meeting to start a society to promote justice and protection of the weak. Muhammad attended with one of his uncles. The members took an oath to stand together on the side of an oppressed person whether he was from Mecca or from abroad. At this meeting Muhammad met Abu Bakr, a young man who would later become his closest friend.

## A Young Merchant

By the time Muhammad had reached twenty, his serious nature and dependability had earned him respect, which helped him develop his career as a merchant, and his relatives frequently asked him to join their caravans to Syria and Mesopotamia. Finally, he was asked to take charge of a caravan by a merchant who was unable to travel. His success in this role led to other similar jobs.

In addition to Muhammad's dependability and intelligence, his strong physical build and good looks made people pay attention to him. The biographer Muhammad Husayn Kaykal describes his striking appearance:

> Muhammad was handsome of face and of medium build, and neither conspicuously tall nor inconspicuously short. He had a large head, very black, thick hair, wide forehead, heavy eyebrows, and large black eyes with a slight redness on their sides and long eyelashes. . . . He had a fine nose, well spaced teeth, a thick beard, a long handsome neck, wide chest and shoulders, light colored skin, and thick palms and feet. He walked resolutely with firm steps. His appearance was one of deep thought and contemplation. In his eyes there lurked the authority of a commander of men.[4]

In spite of his good looks, Muhammad remained a bachelor for longer than what was considered usual at that time, probably because he did not have enough money to support a wife. As an

*Due to his good looks and serious nature, Muhammad earned respect as a young merchant.*

orphan he also had a lower status in the society, which affected his chances of making an advantageous match. When his new job as caravan leader led to greater income, he began to seriously think of marriage.

At that time in Arabia it was normal to marry a person from one's extended family, so it was not considered unusual when his attention was drawn by his first cousin, Umm Hani, the daughter of Abu Talib. His uncle, however, refused permission for the match because he had planned for his daughter to marry a more prominent man. Although Muhammad was probably saddened by this rejection, he and Umm Hani remained good friends.

## KHADIJAH

About 595, when Muhammad was twenty-five, his luck changed upon meeting Khadijah bint Khuwaylid, a distant cousin of his. Khadijah was a wealthy widow and one of the more successful merchants in Mecca. She had been married twice and had a number of children. Her business was to equip caravans to travel to Syria and bring back goods to sell in Mecca. She had learned of Muhammad's good reputation as a caravan leader, so she hired him to take a shipment of her goods to Syria.

When Muhammad returned to Mecca, he went to Khadijah's house to give her the goods he had bought in Syria with the profits from what he had taken there to be sold. She was very impressed with her new assistant's business skills and good looks. Although Khadijah was older than Muhammad (many scholars state that she was forty at that time, but others believe that she was younger because she later had six more children with Muhammad), she went to a friend, Nufaysah, and asked her to serve as a marriage broker. At first Muhammad argued that he did not have enough money to take a wife, but when Nufaysah asked him if he would consider marriage if the woman had beauty, property, and nobility, he said he would be willing. Nufaysah reported this news to

### SLAVERY

Slavery was common in the ancient Middle East, and Jews, Christians, Muslims, and pagans all owned slaves. Some were captives taken in battle. Others were obtained through the abandonment or kidnapping of young children. Sometimes, adults would sell themselves into slavery, and in some cases, parents sold their children. People could also be enslaved if they owed a debt or had committed a crime.

The Koran accepts slavery, but under Islam a slave who believed in Allah was considered the brother of the free man and a superior to pagans. Muhammad urged kind treatment of slaves and condemned harsh treatment of them. He also recommended granting a slave his or her freedom when possible. He said that Islam was open to both free people and slaves.

After Muhammad's death, the early caliphs discouraged and eventually prohibited slavery of Muslims. It also became unlawful for a free Muslim to sell himself or his children into slavery. It became a fundamental principle of Islamic law that the natural condition of humankind was freedom.

Khadijah, who then asked Muhammad to come visit her.

At this meeting she proposed marriage to him, and it was agreed that they would ask permission for the match from their respective families. The marriage was agreed upon, and as a dowry or wedding gift to the bride, Muhammad gave Khadijah twenty female camels. He also freed the slave he had inherited from his father and mother.

Khadijah, in turn, gave her husband the gift of a young slave boy named Zayd. Zayd came to respect and admire Muhammad. Later, when Zayd's father and uncle came to pay a ransom to free him from slavery, the boy chose to stay with Muhammad, who freed him and then adopted him as a son. He became known as Zayd ibn Muhammad, which means Zayd, son of Muhammad.

## A New Household

After the marriage, Muhammad left his uncle's house to move in with Khadijah. The marriage brought Muhammad greater prosperity and prestige as he shared in her successful business. He continued leading caravans to other parts of the Arabian peninsula. His dependability earned

---

### A Sign of Prophecy

After Muhammad became well known, stories were told about his childhood. Some of these described events that predicted his future as a prophet for the Arabs. Although they cannot be proven as fact, they are accepted in the *Hadith* and are part of Muslim beliefs.

One such story relates an incident that occurred when Muhammad accompanied his uncle, Abu Talib, on a merchant caravan trip to Syria. Some scholars say that Muhammad was nine at the time; others say he was twelve. At Basra, one of the stops along the way, a local monk named Bahira invited the merchants to be his guests at a meal. This was unusual because he usually ignored the caravans that passed by. He explained his action, saying that he had seen a cloud overshadowing the caravan, a sign that a prophet must be among the travelers.

Because Muhammad was the youngest in the group, he was told to stay outside and guard the camels. When Bahira asked if all the group was present, he was told that the youngest had been left outside. He then asked that the boy be permitted to enter. One glance at Muhammad's face told him that he was someone special. Then the monk examined Muhammad's back and noticed that there was a mark between his shoulder blades, which he believed was a sign of prophecy. He told Abu Talib to guard his nephew carefully because he was to do great things later in his life.

*Ali, Muhammad's cousin, holds the body of Imam, who died from famine.*

him the nickname of Al Amin, which means a man who can be trusted.

The marriage seems to have been a happy one. Khadijah became Muhammad's strongest supporter, and he often praised her. "Muhammad used to say that she was the best of all the women of her time and that he would live with her in paradise in a house built of reeds and tranquility,"[5] says scholar Maxime Rodinson.

Muhammad and Khadijah had two sons and four daughters, but several did not survive infancy. The first son, al-Qasim, died around the age of two. Muhammad was often called Abu al-Qasim (the father of Qasim), a title he took pride in. A second son, Abd Allah, also died in infancy. The death of his sons was a great loss for Muhammad because in Arab society sons are important to establishing a man's social status. The loss was somewhat softened by his devotion to his four daughters: Zaynab, Ruqayyah, Fatimah, and Umm Kulthum. The girls had a foster brother in Muhammad's young cousin Ali, a son of Abu Talib, whose large family was suffering from the famine that was caused by a serious drought. To help out his uncle, Muhammad adopted the five-year-old boy, who was a year older than his youngest daughter, Fatimah. The four daughters, Ali, and the freed slave Zayd formed Muhammad and Khadijah's immediate family. Both Zayd and Ali thrived in Muhammad's household and would later become leaders in the Muslim movement.

In his thirties, Muhammad's position and reputation in Mecca had improved. He continued to be a businessman, although it is not known whether he helped Khadijah or whether he had his own business. He was known for his kindness to slaves and the less fortunate and gave a large part of his family income to the poor. His own family lived economically. He was a quiet and reserved man, but at home he was devoted to his children and to Khadijah. However, new ideas were stirring in Mecca. Interaction with the Jews and Christians that the Meccan traders met on their frequent caravan trips caused some people to question whether they should continue to worship the many pagan gods rather than one all-powerful deity. A thoughtful man, Muhammad was influenced by these new ideas. His life was about to change.

# 2 A Messenger for God

In spite of his happy family life, business success, and stature in the community, most historians agree that by his late thirties, Muhammad had become increasingly dissatisfied. Some scholars believe he was saddened by not having a biological son, which was considered a source of shame in Arabia at that time. Others believe that one of the factors contributing to his distress was the competitiveness, lack of morality, and inequality that he observed in Meccan society. Historian Ceasar E. Farah describes some of these injustices in his book, *Islam:*

> The wealthy lorded . . . over the poor; the helpless were at the mercy of the strong; greed and selfishness ruled the day; infanticide [the killing of infants] was widely practiced by Bedouins who lacked adequate means of sustenance, and there were numerous other practices prevailing on all levels of Arabian society that had the effect of widening the gulf between the privileged aristocracy and the deprived multitudes of Mecca.[6]

Whatever the reasons, at this time he began to spend a great deal of time in solitude. By the time that Muhammad reached the age of forty, he had begun to experience periods of depression.

## THE FIRST REVELATIONS

It was during this period that Muhammad began to speak of visions that came to him in his sleep. He called these "true visions" and said that they were "like breaking of the light of dawn."[7] As a result of these dreams he became introspective and would often seek solitude in a cave in Mount Hira, just outside the city of Mecca. Dedicating a certain number of nights to meditation, he would take food and water and visit the cave alone. Sometimes he would hear the words "Peace be on thee, O Messenger of God," but when he looked to see who was speaking, he could find no one.

During the Ramadan, the traditional month when the Arabs fasted and reflected on religion, his spiritual retreats to the cave on Mount Hira increased. Muhammad would spend several nights in meditation, returning home for a few days to get supplies. Then he returned to the cave for more contemplation. On the seventeenth night of Ramadan, 610, when he was alone in the cave, he had a surreal experience in which an angel in the form of a man appeared and commanded: "Recite."

*On the seventeenth night of Ramadan, Muhammad stands before a vision of the angel Gabriel, which would inspire the first words of the Koran.*

## The Angel Gabriel

Muhammad fell to his knees and told the angel that he was not a reciter. The angel then embraced him so tightly he could barely breathe and repeated the command. This happened a third time. Finally, the angel released him, and Muhammad found himself speaking what would become the first words of the Koran:

> Read in the Name of your Lord Who has created (all that exists).
> He has created man from a clot (a piece of thick coagulated blood).
> Read! And your Lord is the Most Generous.
> Who has taught (the writing) by the pen.
> He has taught man that which he knew not.[8]

When Muhammad came out of the trance, he was horrified and repelled. Thinking that he was possessed by an evil spirit, he ran to the top of the mountain with the idea of committing suicide, but he was stopped by another vision, which he later identified as the angel Gabriel.

Muhammad later described the experience. "When I was midway on the mountain, I heard a voice from heaven saying: 'O Muhammad! Thou art the apostle of God and I am Gabriel.'"[9] Muhammad goes on to say that looking up, he saw the image of a man that filled the sky. No matter which way Muhammad looked, he saw the image.

Finally, the vision disappeared, and Muhammad returned home, afraid and out of sorts. Trembling, he told Khadijah what he had seen and heard and expressed the fear that he felt that he was going insane or that he was possessed by an evil spirit. He worried that he had become a *kahin*, a seer or fortune-teller who could be possessed by evil spirits. Khadijah reassured him that he was a good man and told him that God did not punish those who were kind and considerate to others. She said she would go for advice to Waraka ibn Nawfal, her elderly cousin who was a Christian convert and a scholar of the Jewish and Christian scriptures.

When Waraka heard what had happened, he proclaimed that Muhammad was the long-awaited prophet for the Arab people. He sent Khadijah home to reassure Muhammad of his sanity. When she told him what Waraka had said, Muhammad's worries were eased, and he returned to the cave to complete his retreat. When his retreat ended, he immediately went to the Ka'aba where he performed a traditional ceremony of walking counterclockwise around the monument seven times, which was the accepted ritual for prayer. At a nearby mosque he met Waraka, who kissed him on the forehead and called him the prophet of the Quraysh.

## MUHAMMAD IS REASSURED

Muhammad received a few more revelations that he believed were from Allah, but

---

### THE INFLUENCE OF JUDAISM AND CHRISTIANITY ON ISLAM

*Experts are divided as to the extent of the influence of Judaism and Christianity on Muhammad's thinking. Both religions were in existence long before Islam, and like Islam they are based on monotheism, or the existence of one god. Author W. Montgomery Watt discusses this influence in his book* Muhammad: Prophet and Statesman:

The form of biblical material in the Koran . . . makes it certain that Muhammad had never read the Bible; and it is unlikely that he had ever read any other books. Such knowledge, then, as he had of Judeo-Christian conceptions must have come to him orally.

Here are various possibilities. He might have met Jews or Christians, and talked about religious matters with them. There were Christian Arabs on the borders of Syria. Christian Arabs or Abyssinians from Yemen may have come to Mecca to trade or as slaves. Some of the nomadic tribes or clans were Christian, and may still have come to the annual trade fair at Mecca. There were also important Jewish groups settled at Medina and other places. Thus opportunities for conversations certainly existed. Indeed Muhammad is reported to have had some talks with Waraka, Kadijah's Christian cousin; and during his lifetime his enemies tried to point to some of his contacts as the source of his revelations.

he and Khadijah kept these occurrences private, discussing them only with their immediate family members. Then for two or three years, the revelations stopped. During this time Muhammad became very depressed, wondering if perhaps he had been an unworthy messenger. Then he received a message that reassured him and pointed him toward his mission:

> By the forenoon (after sunrise).
> By the night when it darkens (and stands still).
> Your Lord, (Oh Muhammad) has neither forsaken you nor hates you.
> And indeed the Hereafter is better for than the present (life of this world).
> And verily, your Lord will give you (all good) so that you shall be well pleased.
> Did he not find you (Oh Muhammad) an orphan and give you refuge?[10]

Now convinced that the revelations came directly from Allah, Muhammad decided to accept the role as prophet to the Arabs. He believed that he had been specially chosen to teach them about his new belief that Allah was the one and only true god, and that he was his messenger. Author Tor Andrae writes, "Mohammad was conscious that since his earliest youth he had been an object of Allah's special care and protection, and that he was especially called. Allah had found him fatherless and poor and gave him a home and riches. But superior to all earthly gifts are the riches of the spirit, the guidance and the Divine commission which the Prophet received through undeserved grace."[11]

Waraka told him that converting the Quraysh would not be an easy task because at first he would be rejected and that his mission would be a dangerous one. Most of the people in Mecca and Arabia were polytheists who believed in many gods and goddesses. It would be very difficult to tell them to reject their traditional beliefs and become monotheists who believed in only one god. Knowing this, Muhammad was very cautious when in 613 he began to tell others about the revelations.

## THE REVELATIONS CONTINUE

The revelations continued for the rest of his life and were later recorded in the Koran, the holy book of Islam. The revelations came in different forms. Muhammad said that sometimes he heard a sound of a bell rather than words, but later he found an idea imprinted in his mind. Other times, he heard actual words, which he memorized and then repeated. At other times the messages came through an angel who took the form of a man. Sometimes the messages came to him instantly. On other occasions he seemed to know when a revelation was about to come. He would lie down and cover himself with a blanket. When the message was over, he would sit up and repeat it.

Receiving the revelations affected him physically. His face might be covered in sweat, even in cold weather, and sometimes he shuddered convulsively. Of these episodes he said, "Never once did I receive a revelation without thinking that my soul had been torn away from me."[12]

*This sixteenth-century Turkish illuminated manuscript depicts Muhammad during meditation receiving a revelation from an angel in the form of a man.*

The earliest revelations that were made before Muhammad was well known were memorized by himself and by his family members. These first teachings, which were in the form of rhymed prose, dealt with the qualities of Allah and life after death. He continued receiving revelations throughout the rest of his life. As Muhammad's fame grew, his followers began to write the revelations on odd bits of fabric, leather, or papyrus, as writing materials were scarce at that time.

The revelations were not immediately published in book form. It was not until after Muhammad's death that the collection of messages were gathered into the Koran, the holy book of Islam. The revelations were organized into verses called

# Pre-Islamic Religion

At the time of Muhammad's revelation that there was only one supreme god, the Arabs were polytheists who worshiped many lesser gods and goddesses at various shrines that were considered to be holy. At the Ka'aba, the most important shrine, there were approximately 360 pagan images, many of which were in the form of stones that were considered to represent the deities. Among these was the image of the god Hubal, which was the largest in the Ka'aba. Although the Arabs also believed in a god they called Allah, by the seventh century the worship of these other gods had become more important.

People came from all over Arabia to worship at Mecca during two pilgrimage seasons in the spring and autumn. Each season lasted for two months during which time fighting was forbidden. The visitors were not allowed to bring food into the courtyard of the Ka'aba, and they had to buy special clothing before they could worship there. Those who were too poor to buy the special clothes had to perform the religious ceremony naked. The most important pilgrimage, called the *hajj*, took place once a year starting at the Ka'aba and proceeding to other shrines in the area. At the end of the *hajj* the pilgrims killed animals as a sacrifice. The land around Mecca, an approximate twenty-mile radius, was considered a sacred area where violence and fighting were prohibited. Although Muhammad abolished the belief in gods other than Allah, he kept many of these traditions as part of Islam.

According to tradition, the worshipers had to walk around the Ka'aba seven times as a form of meditation. The residents of Mecca did not have to wait until a holy season to do this. The rite, called the *tawwaf,* could be performed anytime. In her book *Muhammad: A Biography of the Prophet,* author Karen Armstrong writes:

> The ritual circumambulations which sound so arbitrary and tedious to an outsider, were extremely important in the life of the people of Mecca. It was not a dreary duty which people grudgingly and mindlessly performed. They seemed to enjoy doing it and made it part of their daily lives. They liked to round off a pleasant day's hunting by performing the circumambulations before returning to their homes; they might go along to the nearby market place to drink wine with some . . . companions and then decide to spend the evening making the circumambulations instead, when their drinking companions failed to turn up.

*suras* and were arranged in order of their length rather than in the order Muhammad received them. The earliest revelations were short, but these are placed at the end of the Koran. Later, longer verses are at the first part of the book. There is no narrative or story line to connect the verses. The verses do, however, tell of the consequences of good and bad behavior. Devout Muslims believe that the Koran is the word of God, transmitted by Muhammad through revelations and inspiration.

As Muhammad faced the many problems of his life, he often claimed to receive a revelation from Allah that helped him find solutions. Many of these messages in the Koran became Islamic law, which is followed even today. In one instance a widow appealed to him for help after her husband was killed. According to the custom of the time, all his property was supposed to be inherited by his brother. When Muhammad meditated on the situation, he received a revelation that resulted in detailed rules that are still followed by Muslims. Two-thirds of the estate was to be left to the two daughters, and one-eighth was to go to the wife.

The revelations Muhammad received evolved into his religious teachings, which emphasized a belief in one god and the rejection of all other deities. They also taught that Allah is all powerful and is the creator of the universe. The revelations also warned of a judgment day on which those who have lived according to God's laws would go to Paradise, while Hell would be the fate for those who have been evil. Living according to God's laws involves giving to the poor, helping those less fortunate such as orphans, and being grateful to God. It also involves recognizing Muhammad as the messenger of God.

## THE FIRST FOLLOWERS

Muhammad's first followers were members of his own household, and he taught them how to live and pray. Through a revelation that he believed was from the angel Gabriel, he discerned the postures and movements to follow while praying. He also learned the words "*Allahu, Akbar,* God is Most Great," and the closing of prayer, "*as,-Salamu 'alaykum,* Peace be on you." He taught these things first to Khadijah and then to his ten-year-old cousin Ali, his adopted son Zayd, and his four daughters.

At first the followers called their religion *tazaqqa,* which described a quality that combined charity and generosity toward those less fortunate. Eventually, the religion became known as *Islam,* which means surrendering one's will to Allah, and its followers were called *Muslims,* which describes one who surrenders himself or herself to God.

When Muhammad's close friend Abu Bakr learned about Islam, he immediately became a convert. Muhammad later said, "When I told [Abu Bakr] of it he did not hold back or hesitate."[13] Abu Bakr told people they could trust Muhammad and encouraged them to also become Muslims. Because he had prestige and a good reputation in Mecca, many listened to his advice. One of the young men he helped convert was Khalid ibn Sa'id, the son of an important Quraysh businessman. Because his father was hostile to Islam, Khalid at first kept his religion a secret. Another was a young aristocrat named Uthman ibn Affan who converted to Islam after he had a dream on the way back from a trip to Syria. At first the dream in which he heard a voice saying, "Sleepers awake!" confused him, but when a friend told him about Muhammad, he

*Muhammad's adopted son Zayd (left), one of the first followers of Islam, fights against enemies of the faith.*

accepted the message as an omen that he should convert. He became an avid supporter of Muhammad and married his daughter Ruqayyah. He later became the third caliph, or leader, after Muhammad's death.

Muhammad was disappointed when his uncles Abu Talib, 'Abbas, and Hamzah were not at first interested in converting to the new religion, although their wives did become Muslims. His uncles, however, continued to support and offer him their protection. This was important because in the tribal society it was very difficult for an individual to survive without the protection of his clan. Another uncle, Abu Lahab, was outspoken in his opinion that Muhammad was deluded in his beliefs and even dangerous. Lahab would later become one of Muhammad's worst enemies.

## THE NEW RELIGION APPEALS TO SLAVES AND THE POOR

Although some of the early converts were from the most influential families of Mecca, others were from less aristocratic clans, and some were slaves. Muhammad's message appealed to them for various reasons. Many of the younger followers were rebelling against the conformity of the Quraysh society. Others were attracted by the vision of creating a just society.

Umm Ayman, the freed female slave who had cared for Muhammad when he was a child, converted for these reasons. Zayd, Muhammad's adopted son, was so impressed by this that he asked to marry her even though she was much older than he. Permission was granted, and they were married. The couple's son Usmah was Muhammad's first grandson, and was also one of the first children to become a Muslim. The number of followers continued to grow to about thirty during the first three years of Muhammad's prophethood and included both men and women, many of them young.

The early followers would meet for ritual prayer each morning and evening. The followers memorized the revelations so that they could recite them as part of their prayers. The rite of the *salat,* a form of communal prayer, was also begun. This required the followers to bow down to the ground in homage to Allah and then recite verses from the Koran. The ceremony was performed in the morning and the evening while facing Jerusalem. Some scholars believe that Muhammad chose Jerusalem as a focus because it was the center of the other monotheistic religions, Christianity and Judaism. In addition to praying, the new converts gave gifts to the poor as a demonstration of their faith. Many of the new followers kept their conversions secret for fear of persecution.

## THE QURAYSH ARE SKEPTICAL

About 613 Muhammad received a revelation that told him to warn the people of Mecca that they should become aware of God's perfection. They should recognize Allah as the one supreme being, and they

---

### ABU BAKR

Abu Bakr was perhaps Muhammad's closest friend and associate. He was also among the first people to believe in Muhammad's revelations. Author Sir John Glubb writes, "His real name seems to have been Atik, but he was universally known as Abu [Bakr], the son of Abu Quhafa. . . . [He] was a prosperous merchant, though not among the richest of the Quraysh. He was a man of kindly disposition and was generally popular. Genealogy was a hobby of his and he appears to have been widely accepted as an expert on the subject."

When Muhammad married Aisha, Abu Bakr became his father-in-law, thus strengthening the bond between the two men. Abu Bakr's calm leadership after Muhammad's death impressed the Muslims who elected him to serve as the first caliph or leader. His humility after the election is reported in Ibn Ishaq's *The Life of Muhammad* in which Abu Bakr is reported to have said, "I have been given authority over you but I am not the best of you. If I do well, help me, and if I do ill, then put me to right. Truth consists in loyalty and falsehood in treachery." As caliph he allowed Christian communities to exist in Arabia as long as they recognized the political authority of Islam. He served as leader of the Muslims from 632 until his death two years later in 634.

should stop worshiping idols. He was also told that it was wrong to amass wealth for one's self instead of helping those less fortunate. He took this revelation as an indication that he should begin to preach publicly and urge the wealthy Quraysh to change their ways.

At first the Quraysh leadership either ignored him or thought he was misguided. As his teachings became more public, however, conflicts arose because most people did not want to abandon their old ways. The wealthy merchants thought that Muhammad's teachings were a future threat to their political power. As Muhammad's message appealed to many of the oppressed people of Mecca, there was a danger that someday his power might be greater than that of the Quraysh. Also, many of the Meccans did not want to abandon their old beliefs for something new. They were unsure of the role their old gods would have in the new religion. The wealthy merchants were also offended by some of Muhammad's teachings, especially one

*Muslims bow to the ground in homage of Allah during a rite of* salat, *a communal prayer begun by Muhammad.*

## RAMADAN

Muslims worldwide consider Ramadan one of the holiest months in the year because it was during this time that the prophet Muhammad was first visited by the angel Gabriel and began to receive revelations. Ramadan has its roots in ancient Arabia and is one of the practices that Muhammad continued to observe after he began to receive revelations. It occurs during the ninth month of the lunar calendar, which means that it takes place at a different time each year. During this month, Muslims do not eat or drink between sunrise and sunset. The Night of Power, which in Arabic is called *Lailat-ul-Qadr*, occurs near the end of Ramadan and is celebrated as the exact time of the first revelation in the Koran.

During Ramadan people pray at dawn and fast until sundown. After dark, they shop and visit one another. The festival of *Id-ul-Fitr* comes near the end of the holy month when the new moon appears in the sky over Mecca. Mosques all over the world are informed of this occurrence so that all Muslims can celebrate at the same time. After visiting the mosque to pray, people celebrate by visiting one another and feasting on dates and milk.

about the Last Judgment, which stated that people who were selfish and greedy would be punished after they died.

The new religion created tension in Mecca because it posed a threat to the existing social order. Families were divided as their sons and daughters became followers of Muhammad against their parents' will. Author Karen Armstrong writes: "Muhammad seemed to be turning father against son, brother against brother, and undermining the essential bonds, duties and hierarchy of family life."[14]

In 615, Muhammad received a revelation that told him to ask his Hashim relatives to accept Islam, so he invited about forty of the leaders to a modest meal of roast lamb and milk, which was in stark contrast to the lavish parties that were thrown by the wealthy Quraysh. At the end of the dinner, he began to tell his relatives about his beliefs, but his uncle Abu Lahab broke up the gathering in protest of the Muslim teachings. Muhammad asked the same group back the following night and asked which of them would become followers of Islam. Of those who were present, only Muhammad's ward, thirteen-year-old Ali who had already become a Muslim, accepted the challenge in order to support his guardian.

During these early years of his ministry, Muhammad had been cautious about the people he approached because he was trying to remain on good terms with the leaders of Mecca. He knew that many would be offended by his teachings, especially those about the consequences of selfishness and bad behavior. Many of the Quraysh had amassed great fortunes and were not concerned about the plight of the poor, so they particularly disliked Muhammad's teaching that their greed would be punished in the afterlife. Although he tried to appeal to his clan and to the Quraysh by keeping the traditions such as worshiping at the Ka'aba, he knew that many would reject his message. By 616 he had gathered around himself a moderately small group of devoted followers, but he had not been able to spread his message to a larger audience. As the group began to be more public in their worship of Islam, the Quraysh viewed them with some alarm, but most did not take the new movement too seriously. This, however, was about to change.

# 3 The Early Muslims Meet with Opposition

Although Muhammad's early teachings caused the Quraysh non-Muslims some concern, they had not actively opposed him. As his movement grew, they began to take his teachings more seriously. They wondered what was the role in the new religion of the other deities that had been worshiped in Arabia for many years. They worried that these would be abandoned along with their shrines and symbols and worried that people from other parts of Arabia might not make their pilgrimages to Mecca, which brought prosperity to the Quraysh businessmen. They also asked themselves how Muhammad saw his own role as the leader of the new belief and wondered how a man who claimed to speak directly with God could ever give in to their decisions. Many feared that Muhammad would use his authority as one with whom God spoke as a way to take over the leadership of Mecca.

## AL-LAT, AL-UZZAH, AND MANAT

From his first revelations, Muhammad had insisted that his followers must worship only one god, but he did not specifically attack the other Arabian deities, of which there were many. In 616, however, a crisis arose when he specifically forbade his followers from worshiping three of the most popular ones, the fertility goddesses al-Lat, al-Uzzah, and Manat known as the *banat al-Lah*, or the Daughters of God. The goddesses were represented by large stones, which were housed in shrines within a day or two's journey from Mecca. Al-Lat had a shrine at Taif, and al-Uzzah had a shrine at a site between Taif and Yathrib. Manat's shrine was between Mecca and Yathrib. The ban caused an uproar, as described by biographer Ibn Ishaq: "When the apostle openly displayed Islam as God ordered him, his people did not withdraw or turn against him, so far as I have heard, until he spoke disparagingly of their gods. When he did that, they took great offence and resolved unanimously to treat him as an enemy."[15]

Muhammad's command was unpopular because many of his followers may have assumed that they could worship Allah without giving up their old religious beliefs in other gods. The concept of worshiping only one god was a new idea for many Arabs, but others were not yet ready to break with old traditions.

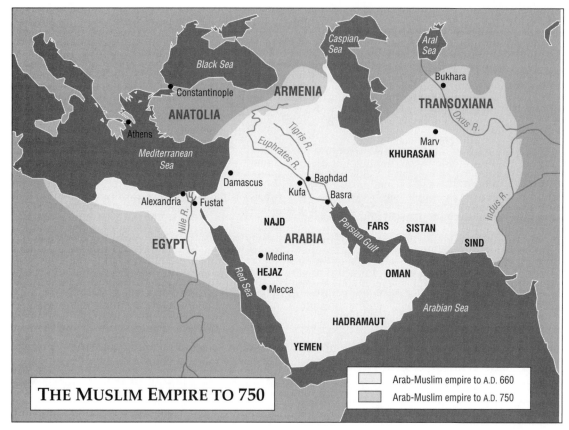

THE MUSLIM EMPIRE TO 750

Arab-Muslim empire to A.D. 660
Arab-Muslim empire to A.D. 750

Another reason for the Quraysh hostility was economic. For many years people from all over Arabia had made an annual pilgrimage to Mecca to worship the idols and to perform the ritualistic processions around the Ka'aba. During the pilgrimages, there were also fairs at which many items were sold, bringing profits to the Quraysh. The wealthy merchants feared that Muhammad's rejection of the ancient idols would discourage the pilgrims from coming to Mecca and would ultimately be bad for business.

The Quraysh leaders met and decided to take action. As a first step they agreed to discredit Muhammad through ridicule. Visitors who came to worship at the shrine were warned that Muhammad was a magician who wanted to create trouble and cause divisions between families. They were advised not to listen to him. Among the people of Mecca, the Muslims were treated as enemies of the state. The result was that many supporters left the movement, and those that remained faced growing hostility from the Quraysh. Almost overnight, the Muslims had become a hated sect.

## THE PERSECUTION CONTINUES

The hostilities against Muhammad and his remaining followers at times became violent. On one occasion, some of the Quraysh followed a group of Muslims to the outskirts of Mecca where they had gone to pray and then attacked them. The Muslims fought back, and one of the Quraysh was wounded.

On another occasion, a delegation of the Quraysh went to Muhammad's uncle Abu Talib and asked him to restrain his nephew. They threatened to fight both uncle and nephew if Muhammad did not moderate his teachings to include worship of the idols. Abu Talib then sent for Muhammad and told him what had occurred. When Muhammad refused to alter his insistence that Allah was the only god, Abu Talib said that he would continue to protect him. The Quraysh were hesitant to follow through on their threats, because they respected Abu Talib's position as chief of his clan and they did not want to challenge the tribal custom in which the leader offered protection to others in the clan.

## THE QURAYSH

The Quraysh were the dominant tribe in Mecca. They were the descendants of a strong leader named Qusayy who took control of the Ka'aba in the fifth century. The tribe was made up of various clans, some of whom were rich and others who were poor. Many of the Quraysh were employed in the business of trade. The most wealthy invested in caravans, which met the ships from India when they landed in Aden. Then they transported the goods to Mecca and other destinations in the Middle East such as Syria, Gaza, or Egypt. After they sold their goods in these places, they would buy local goods, which they brought back to Mecca to sell to the local tribes at the fairs held at the time of the pilgrimages.

The Quraysh ruled Mecca through a council of elders. Muhammad's grandfather, Abdul Muttalib, had served as the head of this council. The system of government was organized in a way that kept any one person or group from becoming too powerful.

Outside Mecca, smaller nomadic tribes called Bedouins lived in the desert and mountains. They did not have farms or land but moved from place to place so that their camels, cattle, goats, and sheep could graze. Although they were loosely organized, most of the tribes followed similar customs. The tribes often fought with one another, but their customs determined how they treated their enemies and prisoners. Although the Quraysh lived in the city, they remembered their desert origins by sending their sons soon after birth to live with Bedouin families where they learned about riding and fighting with swords. They also learned the tribal rules of brotherhood and loyalty, which meant that they would protect the other members of their clans.

*This sixteenth-century Turkish illuminated manuscript depicts Abul-Hakam (left), one of Muhammad's most outspoken opponents, attacking Muhammad, who is leading Muslims in prayer.*

On one occasion when the Quraysh leaders were gathered together at the Ka'aba stirring up opposition to Muhammad, he happened to enter. Although the Ka'aba was the site of many idols, Muhammad continued to honor the site as a place of worship. Author Karen Armstrong writes that "shrines like the Ka'aba and its attendant rituals seem to have answered an important spiritual and psychological need in Arabia. . . . Muhammad felt the mysterious attraction of the Ka'aba all his life."[16] Each time he passed by the Quraysh, they insulted him loudly. The next day, a group surrounded him and grabbed him by his cloak. His friend Abu Bakr intervened and broke up the fight.

One of the most outspoken opponents to Muhammad was a chief known as Abul-Hakam. One day he challenged Muhammad on the street and made insulting remarks about Islam. When Hamzah, one of Muhammad's uncles, was told about the incident, he was furious. Although Hamzah had not accepted the new religion, he considered it an insult to Muhammad and to his tribe. He raced to the Ka'aba where he found Abul-Hakam, and he struck him on the head with his bow declaring that he, too, was accepting Islam. Hamzah's public acceptance of the new religion strengthened Muhammad's position because his uncle was a great warrior whom people respected.

The Quraysh also persecuted Muhammad's followers. Those who were from prominent tribes were beaten by their families, who wanted them to give up the new belief. Those of a lower status were dealt with more violently. An African slave named Bilal was forced by his master to lie on his back in the midday sun with a large rock on his chest. The master vowed to continue this treatment until his slave renounced Allah, which Bilal refused to do. This continued until Abu Bakr passed by and bought Bilal's freedom. Bilal soon became a devoted follower of Islam.

Muhammad became very distressed at the suffering his followers were enduring. As a solution, in 615 he suggested that some of them should immigrate to Abyssinia, a Christian country in eastern Africa, where they hoped to be more accepted. Approximately eighty-three men, along with their wives and children, took this suggestion. Among them was Ruqayyah, one of Muhammad's daughters, and her husband, Uthman. Muhammad and Khadijah, however, remained in Mecca. To avoid drawing the attention of the Quraysh, the emigrants left quietly in small groups of eight or ten. If their families had known of the planned departures, it was feared that they would have stopped it. The Quraysh, fearing that a Muslim community outside their control would be a threat to their power, then sent two ambassadors with gifts of leatherwork to give to the generals and king of Abyssinia to bribe them to make Muhammad's followers return to Mecca. Their efforts were unsuccessful.

## THE SATANIC VERSES

Around this time some biographers recount an incident that for a short time brought a truce between the Quraysh and the Muslims. According to Abu Jafar at-Tabari, a biographer of Muhammad who wrote in the ninth and tenth centuries, Muhammad received a revelation that declared that the three goddesses, al-Lat, al-Uzzah, and Manat, could be worshiped as intermediaries between Allah and man. The Quraysh believed that these messages meant that Muhammad and his followers were accepting the traditional religion and its idols. For a time there was

## ABYSSINIA

Abyssinia, known today as Ethiopia, was a country located in eastern Africa. By 1000 B.C., the area was part of a large empire called the Sabean kingdom. The nobility of Abyssinia traced their ancestry back to the legendary Queen of Sheba, mentioned in the Bible. It is believed that she was a ruler of this kingdom, which was noted for its commerce and wealth. As the distance between Abyssinia and southern Arabia was not great, there was communication between these two areas. The inhabitants of Abyssinia were probably a mixture of east African and southern Arabian descent. Some studies say that the languages of Arabia and the Middle East may be related to that of Abyssinia. The Abyssinians were particularly known for their study of astronomy. It is believed that the black stone that is revered at the Ka'aba was a meteorite brought there from Abyssinia.

By Muhammad's time, Christianity had spread to Abyssinia and was popularly accepted by the royalty and the upper classes. In fact, the country was then ruled by a tolerant Christian king called the Negus.

a truce between the two groups. A short time later, however, Muhammad had another revelation that invalidated the previous message, saying that it had been inspired by Satan, the force of evil. The earlier verses, known as the Satanic verses, were rejected and replaced with others that forbid Muslims to worship the three goddesses. From that time on, Muhammad became uncompromising in his belief in one god, and the persecution of the Muslims resumed. There is continuing controversy regarding the Satanic verses, and many Muslims believe that the incident never happened because it was not cited in many of the early biographies.

Through 616 Muhammad continued to receive revelations that stressed that the followers should worship only one god, Allah, and that no other beings could be objects of worship. This is expressed in sura 73:

> And remember the Name of your Lord and devote yourself to Him with a complete devotion.
> He alone is the Lord of the east and the west. None has the right to be worshiped but He.
> So take him alone as *Wakil* (Protector of your affairs).[17]

The revelations also proclaimed that Muhammad was the prophet who had been chosen to call people to make amends for their wrongdoing and lead them to follow Allah. Muhammad always insisted that he was an ordinary man who did not perform miracles, but as the new religion developed, people began to look upon him as special because he had been chosen to receive the messages. Muhammad's popularity among the Muslims brought about the conversions of some of his harshest critics.

## THE CONVERSION OF UMAR

Near the end of 616 one of Muhammad's most vehement opponents, a young man by the name of Umar ibn al-Khattab, made a conversion to Islam. He had the reputation of being an aggressive man, so his change of mind and acceptance of the peaceful teachings of Islam caused amazement among the Meccans. The conversion occurred on the day he was planning to break into a gathering of about forty Muslims and assassinate Muhammad. When he approached the gathering, a member of his clan approached and told him that before attacking outsiders he should first deal with his sister and her husband, who had recently become Muslims. Umar was

*Muhammad takes flight to the outskirts of Mecca due to criticism and abuse from opponents of Islam.*

so surprised and angry there were Muslims in his immediate family that he rushed to his sister's home and attacked her. When he saw that he had wounded her, his attitude completely changed. He asked to read the Koran for himself and was so impressed that he immediately accepted Islam. Rushing back to the place where Muhammad and his followers were meeting, Umar told the prophet that he had come to believe in his message. The following day, when Umar went to his uncle, the Quraysh leader Abu Jahl, to tell him of his conversion, his uncle angrily rejected him.

Umar became a very devoted follower of Muhammad and a leader in the emerging Muslim movement. While Muhammad and Abu Bakr usually advocated a more gentle approach, Umar was a man who often recommended force. After Muhammad's death, as the second caliph of the movement, he would play an important role in the expansion of Islam.

## THE BOYCOTT

Quraysh leader Abu Jahl was determined to get rid of Muhammad, and therefore imposed a ban on the Hashim and al-Muttalib clans that were related to Muhammad. He convinced the Quraysh to decree that the clans were outlawed and no one could intermarry or trade with them, or even sell them food. The rules of the decree were written out and displayed at the Ka'aba.

For their protection, the members of the two clans, including Muhammad and Khadijah, moved to a street on the edge of town where Abu Talib lived. When Muhammad and his family arrived there, his uncle Abu Lahab, who opposed Islam, moved his family to another part of Mecca. The ban lasted for two years and was very difficult for members of the shunned clans. Muslims from other clans took pity on them and would sneak food and other supplies into the ghetto. The only time Muhammad and his relatives could leave the ghetto was during the four months in the spring and autumn, a sacred time during which they were permitted to go to the Ka'aba to pray. Because any violence was prohibited during these holy months, they were not physically attacked on these outings, but they were often insulted.

The boycott was increasingly unpopular among many in Mecca who did not want to see their friends and relatives suffering from malnutrition. Through the intervention of several sympathetic leaders, it was finally decided to lift the ban and allow the Muslims to reenter Meccan society. When the Muslims who had emigrated to Abyssinia heard that the ban was over, about thirty families, including that of Muhammad's daughter Ruqayyah, returned to Mecca. Another group remained in Abyssinia with Muhammad's cousin Jafar. Although the Muslims were allowed to reenter Meccan society, they were still treated with suspicion and prejudice.

## A YEAR OF SADNESS

The ban had great personal consequences for Muhammad; after two years of suffer-

## THE MUSLIM BELIEF IN PARADISE

*Muhammad's belief that a person's behavior during life would affect his or her fate after death threatened the rich Quraysh who had not shared their wealth with the needy. This was a source of controversy during the early days of Islam. The doctrine taught that there would be a judgment day in which the people who had led sinful lives would be punished, while those who had lived according to the rules of Islam would be admitted to a paradise. Author Tor Andrae in his book* Mohammad: The Man and His Faith *describes Muhammad's conception of paradise.*

Paradise is situated "on high," but whether this is in heaven, or on earth, like the Garden of Eden, is not clearly stated. It is a lovely place, filled with refreshing streams, where leafy bowers provide shade. The redeemed lounge upon divans and cushions, clothed in festive garments of silk and brocade. Gorgeous fruit-trees, pomegranates, bananas, grape-vines, and palms lower their fruit to those who wish to pluck it and furnish shade for those participating in the feast. They are also provided with meat of every kind, and with everything that they desire. Youths as handsome as pearls walk about, serving a delicious drink which does not lead men into speaking foolishly or acting discreditably, nor does it cause headaches or dizziness. For entertainment and in marriage they receive the "black-eyed Houris" of whom Mohammed states that they are virgins, chaste, and especially created by Allah. . . . That the wives and children of believers share in the Joys of Paradise is self-evident for Mohammad, and is especially mentioned in several places.

ing from malnutrition, his wife Khadijah died. Her death was a severe blow, as she had been his first convert and strongest supporter, and he had been faithful to her throughout their marriage. Although he would have a number of wives and concubines after her death, he always referred to her with fondness and affection.

Muhammad did not stay unmarried for long. A few weeks after Khadijah's death, he contracted marriage with a middle-aged widow named Sawdah. Apparently, this was a marriage of convenience and

custom. Because it was an accepted practice for Arab men to be married, remarrying so soon after Khadijah's death was not considered unusual. Sawdah was rather overweight and unattractive, but she was a good housekeeper and was able to care for Muhammad and the two young men, Ali and Zayd, who still lived with him. Muhammad also became engaged to Aisha, the six-year-old daughter of Abu Bakr. The engagement of a very young girl to a much older man was not uncommon in Arabia during this time. In this case it would strengthen the alliance between Abu Bakr and Muhammad.

Not long after losing Khadijah, Muhammad's uncle Abu Talib became ill. Before his death a delegation of Quraysh leaders came to him and asked him to again try to negotiate a truce with Muhammad. However, Muhammad refused to budge from his position that Allah was the only god and that he was Allah's messenger. Muhammad was saddened that in spite of his urging, Abu Talib refused to convert to Islam before he died. His death was a serious blow to Muhammad both personally and politically. Abu Talib had taken on the role of Muhammad's father and guardian when he was an orphan and had played an important role in his life. His uncle's protection as tribal leader of the Hashim had also enabled the new religion to take root. Abu Talib was succeeded by Muhammad's uncle Abu Lahab, who at first promised a similar protection to his nephew. The new leader was not sympathetic to Muhammad's teachings, however, and soon, Muhammad's enemies convinced him to change his mind.

The hostilities increased. On one occasion, neighbors threw a sheep's uterus at Muhammad when he was praying. Another time, an assailant threw sand at his head. Muhammad began to think that leaving Mecca might be a wise course of action. At first he decided to investigate Taif, the agricultural town about fifty miles east of Mecca where many rich Meccans had summer homes. For ten days he visited with local leaders who ridiculed him and stirred up resentment for him among the townspeople. A crowd gath-

*Disciples of Islam surround Muhammad after he returns to Mecca.*

ered, and Muhammad was stoned and chased until he was able to take refuge in a vineyard. Afraid to return to Mecca without protection, he was able to send a message to several Quraysh leaders asking for help. Most refused him, but one, Mutim ibn Adi, agreed to be his protector.

Muhammad was able to return to Mecca, but he was greatly limited in his efforts to convert others to his beliefs. Many of his followers had dropped away, and he was considered a failure by many of the Quraysh. His attempts at conversion were limited to the Bedouin merchants who came to Mecca for trade, but most of these also rejected his message. Muhammad was at the lowest point in his ministry.

## A MYSTICAL DREAM

One night in 620, Muhammad went to the Ka'aba to pray. When he tired, he decided to rest in the northwest section of the shrine in an enclosed area called the *hijr*. He claims he was awakened by a vision of the angel Gabriel, and he felt himself lifted to a magnificent horse called Buruq. He and the angel then flew to Jerusalem where they landed on an outcropping of rock today called the Dome of the Rock. There they were greeted by a crowd of prophets. They climbed up a ladder that reached to heaven and saw a vision of God. The author Karen Armstrong described the importance of the dream in her book *Jerusalem:* "There Muhammad received the final revelation, which took him beyond the limits of human perception. His ascent to the highest heaven had been the ultimate act of *islam*, a return to the unity whence all being derives."[18]

Muhammad later told his followers that in the vision, God had told him that Muslims must pray one hundred times a day. This number was later reduced to five, which has continued to be the practice of Muslims worldwide.

The dream has great importance in Islam and is celebrated on 27 Rajab, the seventh lunar month. It is also the reason why Muslims consider Jerusalem to be the holiest city after Mecca and Medina, and many travel there to worship at the mosque of al-Aqsa, which was built on the Dome of the Rock. For Muhammad, the dream renewed his faith and his determination that Islam should grow and flourish.

# 4 *Hijra*, The Flight to Yathrib (Medina)

Muhammad's position in Mecca had become increasingly dangerous, and his closest associates were also under attack. The growing hostility of the Quraysh continued, and it was becoming more evident that Muhammad and the Muslims were not safe in Mecca.

## HELP COMES FROM YATHRIB

During the annual pilgrimage in 620, Muhammad met six men from Yathrib (now known as Medina), a city located about 250 miles north of Mecca in present-day Saudi Arabia. They were impressed by both Muhammad's message and his personality. The following year, five of the six returned, bringing with them seven others. In all, they represented the different major Arab groups living in Yathrib. They promised Muhammad to serve only Allah, to accept Muhammad as his prophet, and to observe the laws of Islam. This promise is called the First Pledge of al'Aqabah. As proof of their devotion, one of the men said, "We gave allegiance to the apostle that we would associate nothing with God, not steal, not commit fornication, not kill our offspring, not slander our neighbors."[19]

Encouraged by their enthusiasm for Islam, Muhammad wondered if there were more people in Yathrib who would be receptive to his message. When the men returned to Yathrib, he sent along one of his trusted followers to tell the people there about Islam, make converts, and evaluate the political situation.

## YATHRIB

Yathrib was a community split by rivalry and unrest. The population was divided into clans who lived in separate compounds and who were also part of two larger tribes, the Aws and the Khazraj. There were also three Jewish clans. In the past century the different clans had developed rivalries that resulted in escalating violence and fighting. In 618, a few years before the delegation had approached Muhammad, there had been a large battle between the warring factions that involved heavy casualties.

Geography and resources were probably two causes of the tensions. The community of Yathrib was made up of scattered settlements within twenty square miles of oasis in the middle of the desert. The principal agricultural activity was production of dates and cereal grains. Unlike Mecca, which was a commercial hub, most of Yathrib's commerce was involved with the occasional caravans who passed nearby on the trade route to Syria. By the seventh century a growing population was making demands on the community's limited resources.

By June 622, Muhammad's emissary in Yathrib had been successful in gathering converts for Islam, and seventy-five Yathrib Muslims from several different tribes returned to Mecca. Meeting with Muhammad secretly at night, the seventy-three men and two women agreed to live righteous lives and to accept Muhammad as their prophet. They also agreed to fight on his behalf for the followers of Allah. This was important because it meant that the Muslims of Yathrib would offer protection to people who were not related to them, thus breaking the long Arab tradition of loyalty only to those of one's clan and family. In return, Muhammad pledged his loyalty to Yathrib. One by one, the Muslims from Yathrib walked past Muhammad, each striking his hand to show their loyalty. This meeting is known as the Second Pledge of al'Aqabah, or the Pledge of War. From that time, the Muslims of Yathrib were known as the Helpers, and the Meccan followers of Muhammad were known as the Companions.

## YATHRIB CHANGES MUHAMMAD'S LIFE

*Thomas Carlyle, the nineteenth- and early-twentieth-century British author and philosopher, wrote and lectured about Muhammad in a series called Lectures on Heroes. He believed that Muhammad was responsible for transforming a group of different nomadic tribes into an Arab nation united in their belief in one god. Carlyle considered Muhammad's move to Yathrib as a turning point in this transformation. The following is an excerpt from his essay, "The Hero as Prophet," published in 1901:*

In the thirteenth year of his mission, finding his enemies all banded against him, forty sworn men, one out of every tribe, waiting to take his life, and no continuance possible at Mecca for him any longer, [Muhammad] fled to the place then called Yathrib, . . . the place they now call Medina, or 'Medinat al Nabi, the City of the prophet. . . . It lay some 200 miles off, through rocks and deserts. . . . The whole East dates its era from this Flight, *Hegira* as they name it: the year 1 of this Hegira is 622 of our era, the fifty-third of [Muhammad's] life. . . . Now, driven . . . out of his native country, . . . the wild Son of the Desert resolved to defend himself, like a man and Arab. . . . Ten years more of this [Muhammad] had; all of fighting, of breathless impetuous toil and struggle with what result we know.

*Muhammad rides his camel, Qaswa, across the desert to Medina with Abu Bakr.*

## *HIJRA*, OR MIGRATION TO YATHRIB

Muhammad decided to emigrate to Yathrib, and in July and August 622, about seventy Muslim families left Mecca to make the journey. Among the first to go were his closest relatives. For many of the Muslims, moving away from Mecca was a difficult decision, as they left behind friends, family, and businesses in addition to the protection of their clans. It was also a potentially risky decision because of possible retaliation from the Quraysh, who feared that the Muslims could threaten

Mecca if they became a strong force in a new community. To avoid problems, the immigrants left quietly in small groups that met outside the town. Muhammad and Abu Bakr were the last to leave, so as not to arouse suspicion.

In August 622, Muhammad became even more vulnerable when Mu'tim, his protector, died and he was left without protection. With the threat of retaliation removed, the Quraysh called a special meeting to decide how to deal with him. Because the new religion posed a possible threat to the safety of Mecca and the stability of the social order, the Quraysh decided to murder Muhammad, thinking that the religious movement would collapse without his leadership. It would be necessary to find a way to do this without angering the remaining members of the Hashim clan, who would seek revenge for his assassination. The Quraysh came up with a clever plan in which each of the remaining clans would choose a young man as a representative to make up the group that would assassinate Muhammad. That way no one clan could be held responsible, and it would not be possible for the Hashim to take revenge on so many groups.

The chosen group gathered outside Muhammad's house, but when they heard Muhammad speaking with the women of his household, they held back, feeling it would be wrong to kill him in the presence of his family. They decided to wait until morning when he left the house. The following morning they realized they had been tricked when his cousin Ali walked out wearing Muhammad's clothing. During the night Muhammad had escaped through a back window and had fled the town in the company of Abu Bakr and a guide. The Quraysh then offered a reward of one hundred female camels to the person who brought him back to Mecca, dead or alive.

## A Welcome at Yathrib

The trip to Yathrib was dangerous because Muhammad and his friend Abu Bakr traveled without tribal protection. For the first three days, the two men eluded capture by hiding in a cave outside the city. When they continued their journey, they stayed away from the known routes to avoid capture.

The Muslims who had emigrated from Mecca had been eagerly awaiting Muhammad's arrival. Having heard of his

## The Muslim Calendar

The Muslim calendar begins with the first day of 622, the year when Muhammad and his followers made the *hijra* or emigration to Medina. The letters A.H., which stand for *anno Hegirae* or after the *hijra* in Latin, follow the date. At his last pilgrimage, Muhammad ordered Muslims to observe the lunar calendar, which is based on the cycles of the moon. Months are 29 or 30 days long. Twelve lunar months, however, are approximately 11 days short of the solar year of 365 days. The result is that a month that falls in the summer one year rotates gradually back into spring, then winter, then fall. The Muslim holy holidays including Ramadan move from one time of year to another and are celebrated 11 days earlier than the year before. Over a period of time, the holidays occur in different seasons.

*Muhammad and Abu Bakr eluded their Quraysh captors by hiding in a cave covered by a spider's web.*

departure from Mecca, they were anxious when they had not received further news about him. Finally, news arrived that Muhammad and Abu Bakr had reached Qoaba, a settlement on the edge of the oasis of Yathrib. Historians differ as to the date of Muhammad's arrival in Yathrib, some saying it was June 28, 622, and others saying it was September 24, 622.

Muhammad's first task was to decide where to live. As a man of faith, he said he would leave the decision to Allah. He decided to give his camel, Qaswa, her lead, declaring he would accept the place where she stopped as the site for his future home. The camel stopped and fell to her knees near the middle of an oasis at a section of land that belonged to two orphaned brothers who were date farmers.

Muhammad bought the land from them and ordered a structure to be built on the site. This would serve as a center for the Muslim community, a place of worship and also as a home for his family.

Followers from both Mecca and Yathrib worked to build the structure that later came to be known as a mosque, and Muhammad also reportedly helped in the construction. The construction took close to a year. The building was made of mud bricks and had a large rectangular courtyard for group worship and other gatherings. It was here that Muhammad also gave speeches to his followers and conducted business. Adjacent to the structure were two small buildings for Muhammad's wife, Sawdah, who had remained in Mecca, and Aisha, his young fiancée.

As Muhammad took more wives, additional rooms were added for them. He did not have an apartment of his own and stayed with a different wife each night. The rooms of the mosque were simply built. Instead of doors, some openings had strips of cloth to provide protection.

Muhammad wanted to find a way to call the people to prayer at the same times each day. One of his followers had a dream that a man with a loud voice should cry out "'al-Llahu Akbar," meaning "God is great," three times to call the faithful to prayer. Muhammad liked this idea and chose Bilal, the slave who was freed by Abu Bakr, to climb to the top of the tallest building each day before dawn. As the sun rose, he called the people to prayer crying out, "'al-Llahu Akbar. 'al-Llahu Akbar. 'Al-Llahu Akbar. I bear witness that there is no God but al-Llah, I bear witness that Muhammad is the

## THE MOSQUE

Shortly after Muhammad's death, Muslims began to build places of worship called mosques. A model for the earliest mosques was the courtyard of Muhammad's house in Medina, which was built in A.D. 622. A little later mosques became more complex and ornamental in design.

Mosques are not built according to a definite pattern, although there are some elements that are mandatory. These include the *qibla,* which indicates the direction toward which a person orients himself or herself for the *salat,* or prayer of Islam. The *qibla* always faces toward Mecca and is placed in a niche in the wall called the *mihrab.* Many Muslims consider the *mihrab* the holiest place in the mosque. The *mihrab* may be built of wood or masonry and is usually highly decorated. The mosque must have a roofed area in front of the *mihrab,* and the wall in which it is placed can have no doors.

The *minbar* is the place in the mosque where the religious leader conducts Friday prayers. Usually it is placed near the *mihrab.* Other elements in the mosque are the *kursi,* a desk on which the Koran is placed and a desk for the reader; carpets; lights, both candles and lamps; incense; and water in the courtyard for the worshipers to drink and clean themselves. After Muhammad's death, mosques became very important symbols and often were the first structures built when Muslim conquerors established themselves in a new place.

When entering a mosque, a person removes his or her shoes and gives blessings to Muhammad and his family. People speak in low voices, and for Friday services nice clothing is worn. Traditionally, women have not been welcome in mosques, but today many mosques segregate men and women, although this is not required in the Koran.

apostle of God. Come to prayer. Come to prayer. Come to divine service. Come to divine service."[20]

## MARRIAGES AT YATHRIB

After his new home was ready, Muhammad sent for the women of his family, who had stayed behind in Mecca. A few months after the dedication of the mosque, Muhammad decided that it was time to marry Aisha, who was now nine years old.

For a man in his fifties, Muhammad was still good looking. Author Maxime Rodinson describes the prophet's appearance around the time of his marriage to Aisha:

> We are told that he was of medium height, with a large head but a face that was neither round nor at all plump. His hair was slightly curly and his eyes were large, black and well-opened beneath long lashes. His complexion was fair with a tendency to ruddiness. He had only a few fine hairs on his chest while those on his hands and feet were in contrast, very thick, and his beard luxuriant. He was big-boned and broad-shouldered and walked with a strong, swinging stride, like one going downhill.[21]

Although Aisha did not have any choice in the marriage, she accepted this arrangement because she had seen her parents treat Muhammad with love and respect. Also, in seventh-century Arabia, marriages were often arranged to form political alliances between tribes or families. Years later, when talking about her wedding, she said, according to the early biographer Ibn Sa'd, "I was playing on a see-saw and my long streaming hair was disheveled. They came and took me from my play and made me ready."[22] Her hair was combed, and she was dressed in a wedding dress of red-striped material and was adorned with jewelry and ornaments. Then she was led to Muhammad. A simple ceremony followed during which both bride and groom drank from a bowl of milk to symbolize their union. There was no further wedding feast or celebration.

After the marriage she moved into the rooms that had been built for her, where Muhammad visited her often to watch her play with her toys and dolls. Sometimes he would join the games she and her friends played. It is believed that the marriage was not consummated until Aisha reached puberty. The marriage solidified the relationship between Aisha's father, Abu Bakr, and Muhammad. Many of Muhammad's other marriages and those of his daughters had a political basis as well. Although Aisha was young, she was very observant. In accounts she made after Muhammad's death, she spoke of his concern about the Companions' homesickness for Mecca and their hard adjustment to their new lives during their first months in Yathrib.

## CHALLENGES IN YATHRIB

Although they were a closely knit group of around fifteen hundred followers, the

*An illustration from 1774 depicts the great mosque Muhammad built in Medina.*

Muslims from Mecca faced many challenges during their first years in Yathrib. The Companions from Mecca knew that they could not depend forever on the goodwill of the Helpers for financial support. Although Muhammad had arranged for some of the Helpers to adopt Companions until they were established in the new community, it was expected that the new arrivals would not be a burden. For many, work was difficult, as most of the Companions had been bankers and merchants in Mecca. Making a living in the farming community of Yathrib was not something they could easily do, even if fertile land had been available. Yathrib had little opportunity for trade, which was monopolized by Mecca. Having left their possessions in Mecca, most were penniless. Soon after their arrival, many of the Meccans were starving. Even Muhammad's family suffered from hunger, their usual diet being dates washed down with water.

The position of Muhammad and the Muslims in the community also needed to be defined. As Yathrib had no formal government, the traditions of clans and tribal affiliations determined how disputes were handled. At first, the Muslims from Mecca were considered just another clan. The people of Yathrib, although friendly, continued to follow many of their old customs, and although many had converted to Islam, not all were equally passionate about the new religion. Some of the less enthusiastic began to follow Abdullah ibn Ubbayy, a tribal chief who was highly respected and was considered by many to be the unofficial leader of Yathrib.

## THE CONSTITUTION OF YATHRIB

Muhammad needed to assert his claim as leader, and so drafted a document known as the Constitution of Yathrib. The exact date of this document is unknown, but many scholars believe that it comes from the early Muslim period in Yathrib with some clauses added at a later time.

The constitution begins, "In the name of god the Merciful, the compassionate! This is a writing of Muhammad the prophet between believers and Muslims of Quraysh and Yathrib . . . and those who follow them and are attached to them and who crusade along with them. They are a single community distinct from other people."[23]

The articles that follow state that each clan was responsible for protecting the other members of the greater community, an important provision because there was no police in Yathrib at that time. For the emigrants from Mecca who had left their tribes behind, the protection provided by the clans of Yathrib was essential for their survival. With the constitution, the Muslim community of believers called the *umma* replaced the old concept of tribal affiliation and its unwritten rules of protection and retribution. This was a revolutionary idea in seventh-century Arabia. Muhammad hoped to replace the institution of the tribe with membership in the Muslim community.

Although the constitution mainly referred to Arabs, it also defined the rights and duties of the Jewish residents. Most of the Jews in Yathrib were better educated than the Arabs, and many had wealth from trade. Muhammad hoped that they would recognize him as a leader. He received a revelation that clarified his position in regard to the Jewish clans. Historian Sir John Glubb cites part of the revelation that appeared in the agreement between the Companions, the Helpers, and the Jews. "To the Jew who follows us belong help and equality. He shall not be wronged nor his enemies aided. . . . The Jews have their religion and the Muslims have theirs."[24] All who agreed to the constitution, Jewish or Arab, were bound to help one another if there was an attack on Yathrib.

Muhammad's arrival in Yathrib marked a change in his role as religious leader, as he was almost immediately drawn into political decisions. Karen Armstrong writes, "As Muhammad became more and more of a statesman, he was in the deepest sense still inspired and he was gradually

## THE KORAN

*For Muslims, the Koran is the foremost authority for faith and practice both in religion and in secular life. Although it has been translated into many languages, only the Arabic version is considered to be the word of God. The Arabic verses of the Koran have often been written using beautiful calligraphy, which is a work of art. Many Muslims memorize the verses and use a page or fragment of the Koran as an amulet, which they wear on their bodies to ward off evil influences and illness. Out of respect, the Koran is never placed on the ground.*

*Author Karen Armstrong writes of the development and significance of the Koran in her book* Muhammad: A Biography of the Prophet:

Non-Muslims . . . will find the [Koran] a valuable source of information about Muhammad. Even though it was not officially compiled until after his death, it can be regarded as authentic. Modern scholars, who have been able to date the various *suras* with reasonable accuracy, point out that, for example, the earliest parts of the [Koran] refer to the special problems that Muhammad encountered while his religion was still a struggling little sect and that these would have been forgotten later, when Islam was an established and triumphant religion. In the [Koran], therefore, we have a contemporaneous commentary on Muhammad's career that is unique in the history of religion: it enables us to see the peculiar difficulties he had to contend with, and how his vision evolved to become more profound and universal in scope.

evolving a solution that would bring peace to the Arabs."[25] The tone of the revelations he received at this time began to reflect what was going on in Yathrib, and many of them evolved into laws and regulations for the new society. The Muslims used these revelations as a blueprint from God to create a new kind of community that was based on the principles of Islam.

As Muhammad solidified his position in Yathrib, the city became known as Medina or *Medinat al Nabi,* or City of the Prophet. Muslims consider their religion to have begun with the *hijra* to Medina, and 622 became the first year of the Islamic calendar. A.H. is placed before the date to designate "anno Hegirae," a Latin phrase meaning "after the *hijra.*"

## THE JEWS OF MEDINA

At first Muhammad hoped to unite the Muslims with the Jews of Medina who were, along with Christians, called People of the Book because like the Muslims, they, too, had been sent scriptures from God. It is believed that this is the reason he instructed his followers to face in the direction of Jerusalem when they prayed. He also set Friday, the eve of the Jewish Sabbath, as a time of worship for Muslims. Muslims also followed some of the same dietary restrictions as the Jews. They did not eat pork or meat from animals that had died a natural death. In spite of these concessions, the Jews did not accept Muhammad as a prophet as he had hoped.

Muhammad admired and respected the Jewish prophets Moses and Abraham, and the Koran relates stories about them. As the Jews heard the stories, however, they noticed that they differed from the biblical versions they knew. Soon, some of the Jews began to come to the worship services to ridicule the Muslims, causing disagreements and fights.

As conflict with the Jewish community developed, Muhammad received a revelation that caused an important change in Islam. Jerusalem would no longer be the city Muslims would pray toward. Instead they would face Mecca. This symbolic change demonstrated a new Muslim sense of identity that emphasized the religion's Arab roots.

During the first year in Medina, Muhammad's position was still uncertain, as many of the people living there had not yet converted to Islam. During this period, however, Muhammad had gained power and developed his abilities as a statesman and politician. His next challenge was to look beyond the boundaries of Medina to find a way to finance his growing community.

# 5 Raids and Battles

By 623 and 624 the Muslims were beginning to look beyond Medina to find means of survival. The shortage of food was a serious problem, and even Muhammad and his own family suffered from hunger. Because the Muslims from Mecca were businessmen who found it difficult to adapt to the farming economy of Medina, finding another source of income had become an urgent need. Attacking the rich caravans that traveled to and from Mecca became a lucrative and alluring solution to their problems.

Not long after he had arrived in Medina, Muhammad had received a revelation that gave the Muslims permission to fight if they were righting a wrong. The message promised that God would protect them and lead them to victory if their ultimate goal was to create a just society. Muhammad believed that he and the Companions had been severely persecuted by the Quraysh who had driven them from their homes in Mecca, resulting in a loss of their properties and livelihoods. In view of the revelations he had received, he believed that seeking retaliation for these abuses was not unjust. He also knew that to gain restitution for these wrongs, he and the Companions would eventually have to challenge the Quraysh; however, to attack them openly at that time would be a disaster. He decided that at the present time, a safer and more profitable option would be to raid the Quraysh caravans that passed about sixty miles to the south on their way to Yemen and Syria. The caravans were known for their rich cargo of silk, weapons, cereals, and oil. As they were usually guarded by only a few merchants, they would be easy prey. In 623, about seven months after the Muslims had arrived in Medina, Muhammad decided to make a strike.

## RAIDS

In seventh-century Arabia, raiding unfriendly or weaker tribes was a common practice that brought prestige to one's group. Using the element of surprise, the raiders would invade an enemy's territory and capture camels, cows, and other forms of wealth. Usually, these attacks were carried out without bloodshed, for if people were killed, it could spark retaliation. Maxime Rodinson writes:

> Private wars were a perfectly accepted custom. In this society, in

which the idea of a state was wholly unknown, each petty chieftain was in a position to send his men to attack any objective he cared to set them. All he had to do was to take the consequences, which, if he was wise, he measured well beforehand. There was therefore nothing, beyond possible considerations of expediency, to prevent Muhammad from indulging in such warlike activity. His people, for the most part, followed him as a matter of course.[26]

The first raids between June and October of 623 were under the leadership of Muhammad's uncle, Hamzah, or a warrior named Ubaydah ibn al-Harith. Although these raids were unsuccessful, the Quraysh were surprised that the Muslims had the courage to attack them, and they made safeguards to protect their goods. In September 623, when Muhammad learned that a large caravan of twenty-five hundred camels would pass near Medina, he decided to lead the raid himself. The Quraysh's precautions paid off, however, and the caravan eluded capture.

These first raids mainly involved the Companions from Mecca, the original Muslims. Although in the Second Pledge of al'Aqabah the Helpers in Medina had promised to defend Muhammad and his followers from their enemies, they had not agreed to take part in aggressive attacks. Also, some of the Muslims from Mecca were reluctant to fight the Quraysh because they were still clinging to tribal loyalties and feared that they might accidentally harm a member of their own clan.

## THE RAID AT NAKHLAH

As winter neared, the Quraysh stopped sending their caravans to Syria and only sent them to Yemen in the south, bypassing Medina. Therefore, in January 624, during the pagan month of Rajab, Muhammad decided to send a small raiding party to attack the Quraysh closer to their home.

Persuading his followers from Mecca to attack their relatives and friends had been one of Muhammad's most difficult tasks because doing so broke the sacred ties of tribal relationships. His aim was to destroy tribal loyalties, replacing them with a commitment to Islam. Author Alfred Guillaume writes, "By the preaching of war as a sacred duty, Muhammad gradually induced his followers to attack the Meccans."[27]

According to the rules of the pagan religion practiced throughout most of Arabia, fighting was strictly forbidden during holy months. Muhammad ignored this rule because he no longer observed the holy months that were part of the pagan religion. Muhammad sent a raiding party of nine men who went to Nakhlah, which was on the road between Mecca and Taif, to make a surprise attack on a Quraysh caravan that was returning from Yemen.

When they found the caravan, the raiders at first joined it, pretending to be pilgrims going to Mecca. Because the Quraysh felt relatively safe, they were unprepared for the attack in which one guard was killed and two were captured. One guard managed to escape.

There was both celebration and anxiety when the Muslims returned to Medina

*In September 623, Muhammad convenes with the Companions from Mecca to raid a large Meccan caravan.*

with the prisoners and the caravan. Some of the people of Medina were upset that Muhammad had broken the rule against fighting during Rajab. Others were worried that the Quraysh would retaliate. After all, the Quraysh had suffered a blow to their prestige. It was inevitable that they would soon seek revenge.

When he saw the people's response, Muhammad denounced the raid and refused to take any of the spoils. Author Karen Armstrong describes Muhammad's change of heart in her book *Muhammad: A Biography of the Prophet:*

We must remember that pagan practice and enthusiasms probably differed widely throughout Arabia. He was unlikely to have had any idea that the Medinans felt so strongly about this pagan practice, and when he saw the distress of the Helpers when the raiding-party returned, he realized that he had unwittingly trampled on their religious sensibilities. There was no point in holding obstinately to his course. If the people wanted to keep the sacred months they should be allowed to do so, because there was

## THE CONCEPT OF *JIHAD*, OR HOLY WAR

A short time after the raid at Nakhlah, Muhammad received a revelation that clarified for him the legitimacy of fighting for a just cause. The message revealed that while it was inappropriate to fight during the holy months, it was worse to keep people from following God as the Meccans had done by keeping the Muslims from worshiping at the Ka'aba. Thus, Muhammad's actions against the Quraysh were justified in the eyes of God.

The revelation is written in *Sura, Verse 39* of the Koran: "Permission to fight (against disbelievers) is given to those (believers) who are fought against, because they have been wronged; and surely, Allah is able to give them (believers) victory."

The Islamic concept of *jihad* began to emerge around this time. The word has come to mean "holy war," but it also implies a moral, spiritual, and intellectual struggle to create a just society where the weak and poor are not taken advantage of. Fighting back against injustice is permissible. At times fighting and killing might become a part of *jihad*, but the concept also has broader implications, which include a person's struggle to remove evil and wrongdoing from his or her personal life and from society.

nothing in this practice that offended his religion of the one God.[28]

The renunciation, however, created depression among those who had participated in the raid because they felt they had acted wrongly.

## MUHAMMAD GETS INVOLVED

Up to this time Muhammad had led raids but had not personally engaged in any of the fighting, but he knew that to establish his authority as leader, he would soon have to fight. A decisive victory was needed to maintain his prestige. The wealth that would come from a successful battle was also needed. Success depended on catching the Quraysh by surprise.

In March 624, the Muslims learned that the Quraysh leader Abu Sufyan would be leading a large caravan of over one thousand camels close to Medina on the way back from Syria. This was one of the most important caravans of the year and was bringing back to Mecca a valuable cargo of merchandise. If the Muslims could capture the caravan, they would profit considerably. Three hundred fifty Muslims volunteered to attack the caravan. They did not have armor and took turns riding the seventy camels and the two horses that they were able to round up. Muhammad reportedly shared his camel with Ali and his adopted son Zayd.

The Muslims plotted to ambush the caravan at Badr, a watering hole near the Red Sea about eighty miles from Medina. They sent two Bedouin trackers ahead to scout and learned the caravan was expected the following day. When Muslim forces had advanced to a short distance from the wells at Badr, Muhammad and his leaders decided to move forward and surround the wells, cutting off the enemy's access to water.

## THE FIGHTING BEGINS

In seventh-century Arabia, combat between two opposing armies was very different from war as we know it today. Rather, it was more of a contest between the two sides. The commander or his lieutenants stepped forward to challenge the enemy to a single combat. Sometimes the commander would lead the charge. At any rate, his main job was to set an example of heroism for his men.

According to this custom, the Quraysh leader challenged the Muslims to send out three of their warriors to fight. Muhammad called upon his uncle, Hamzah, his cousin and son-in-law Ali, and a third man named Ubaydak ibn al Harith, who was killed. The other two were excellent swordsmen who quickly killed their adversaries. The deaths weakened the

*A raiding party sent by Muhammad joins the Quraysh, whom they would fight during Rajab.*

*Muhammad leads his army to the wells at Badr to cut off the Quraysh from drinking water.*

confidence of the Quraysh, who may have believed that Muhammad, who had claimed that Allah was his protector, had supernatural assistance. Muhammad had told his men that each one killed that day in battle would be admitted to Paradise.

After fierce fighting, the Muslims won. It was estimated that the Quraysh had lost between forty-nine and seventy men, while the Muslims only had fourteen casualties. In addition, many of the Quraysh were taken as prisoners. The ransoms paid for the prisoners' release brought needed wealth to Medina. More important, the battle of Badr let the Quraysh know that the Muslims had grown strong and powerful.

## MARRIAGES IN MEDINA

When Muhammad returned from Badr, he learned that his daughter Ruqayyah had died. Her husband, Uthman, was very sad, so Muhammad offered his other daughter, Umm Kulthum, to him as a wife. Muhammad grieved for Ruqayyah and often visited her grave with his youngest daughter, Fatimah, who was about twenty. About this time he decided that it was time for her to get married too and decided she should marry his cousin and ward, Ali, who was at first reluctant because he was very poor. Before her marriage, Fatimah had served as a sort of hostess for her father, but after the marriage, she had to adjust to living in pov-

erty. Ali worked as a water carrier, and Fatimah worked grinding grain.

Muhammad also decided to take another wife at this time. He chose a woman named Hafsah, the daughter of Umar, who had been widowed when her husband was killed at Badr. She was eighteen, beautiful, and educated. She knew how to read and write, qualities that were rare for a woman in seventh-century Arabia. The wedding took place in 625. By marrying Hafsah he was now allied by marriage with Umar, one of his closest friends.

## SEVENTH-CENTURY WARFARE

*In seventh-century Arabia armies as we know them today did not exist. The preparations for war involved the entire community and made secrecy virtually impossible. The Koran taught that the only just war was one of self-defense, but if Muslims had to fight, they were to do so with absolute commitment so that the war could be quickly ended.*

*Author Sir John Glubb, in his book* The Life and Times of Muhammad, *describes the type of force that was in existence at the time of Muhammad's military expeditions:*

It must be remembered that no such thing as an army existed, nor was there anything in the nature of an establishment of officers or other ranks. In the simple communities of Arabia, every man was automatically a fighter.

When the chief of a tribe, or in this case the [Prophet], ordered a raid, the word had to be passed round to all the men of the community. Each man had to provide himself with a horse or camel, or arrange to share a camel with a friend or relative, for a camel could carry two. Every man had also to provide himself with food for the campaign, for there was no organization for the transport and issue of rations. Each man would also require a good water-skin, perhaps two, and his weapons, sword, lance, and bow and arrows. All this kept the whole community in a bustle of activity, speculation and rumor for a considerable time, perhaps two or three weeks. During this period, casual travelers, merchants or bedouins inevitably carried news of the preparations to the intended victims.

Aisha became friends with Hafsah, who was close to her age, and the two younger wives would often gang up against Sawdah. One day they teased the older wife by telling her that a false prophet called the *dajjal* had come to Medina. When Sawdah heard this, she became very frightened and hid. The girls ran to tell Muhammad what they had done, and he had to rescue the older woman from her hiding place.

After the battle of Badr, more people came to Medina to accept Islam. Many of these were very poor and had no place to live, and many of the newcomers had to take shelter at the mosque. Often there was little food, and the new settlers had to resort to what was available. Muhammad allowed the followers to eat certain foods that he would not eat himself, such as the large lizards that were abundant in Medina.

*Muhammad pledges his daughter Fatimah to his cousin Ali.*

## VIOLENCE AGAINST THE NON-MUSLIMS

Starting in 624, Muhammad's treatment of people who criticized Islam led to one of the darkest and most disturbing episodes of his life. When he returned to Medina after the battle of Badr, he decided to take action against the remaining Medinans who had not become Muslims.

His first move was against a pagan woman poet who had written verses criticizing him. He publicly complained about her and asked if someone would

get rid of her for him. That evening one of her clan members went to her house and killed her while she was sleeping. The next month another elderly poet who had criticized Muhammad was also killed in his sleep.

Muhammad began to also attack the Jews, many of whom were ethnic Arabs who had been converted to Judaism centuries earlier. He had been very irritated by the Jews' decision to not join the force that went to Badr and was also disappointed that they had not converted to

Islam. He started with the clan that was considered the weakest and least likely to fight back. The clan, the Qaynuka, was mainly made up of craftsmen and goldsmiths who were also allied with Abdullah ibn Ubbayy, a Medinan chief who had converted to Islam, but who was a continuing threat to Muhammad's authority.

Muhammad soon found an excuse to attack the clan a few months after the battle of Badr, when a Muslim girl was insulted by some young Jews in the marketplace. In retaliation a blockade was placed around the clan's neighborhood so that they could not receive food. When the clan surrendered after the fifteen-day siege, Muhammad initially wanted to put them to death. However, Abdullah ibn Ubbayy intervened on their behalf, and instead of being killed, the Jews were given three days to get out of Medina, leaving their possessions behind. Their wealth was divided among the Muslims, and Muhammad claimed for himself one-fifth of the confiscated property.

Muhammad's authority was growing and so was his vengeance against those who disagreed with him. One of the most violent acts he ordered was against a half-Jewish poet of the Nadir clan who while in Mecca had written poems criticizing Muhammad. When he returned to Medina, a group of Muslims posing as traitors to the Muslim cause lured him to a secret meeting and killed him, bringing his head back to Muhammad as a trophy.

While Muhammad was dealing with the non-Muslims in Medina, he also worried that the Quraysh would soon seek retaliation for their defeat at Badr.

## THE QURAYSH STRIKE BACK AT UHUD, MARCH 625

In Mecca the Quraysh under the leadership of Abu Sufyan were making preparations to return to fight the Muslims. In addition to the Quraysh, the army of about three thousand men was made up of troops from neighboring tribes and a large number of slaves. They also had two hundred horses and three thousand camels. A dozen or so women accompanied the troops and encouraged them by beating tambourines and singing.

The army marched ten days and on Thursday, March 21, 625, camped at the hill of Uhud a few miles north of the oasis of Medina. When they heard of the advance, the residents of Medina took refuge inside their homes, taking with them their livestock and tools. They watched in dismay as the camels and horses of the Meccan army ate their crops.

On Friday morning, after the afternoon prayers, the Muslim army of about one thousand men set out to meet the Quraysh who both outnumbered them and who had better equipment. Halfway to Uhud, Muhammad stopped and sent back the youngest warriors, fearing for their safety. The men loyal to Abdullah ibn Ubbayy also turned back, leaving a force of seven hundred, who then pitched camp in a protected rocky area.

The following morning, an all-out war broke out. The Quraysh troops were urged to fight by the women who accompanied them, who called for revenge, shouting the names of the men who had died at Badr.

*On March 21, 625, at Uhud, Muhammad's army met the much larger Quraysh army.*

## MUHAMMAD IS WOUNDED

For the first time in any of the skirmishes, Muhammad himself was drawn into the combat and was soon wounded when a stone split his lip and broke one of his teeth. Another stone smashed a part of his helmet and cut his cheek. Then, one of the Quraysh knocked him backward into a

hole. He was so badly shaken that he had to be helped back to safety.

Meanwhile, many Muslims were killed including Muhammad's uncle Hamzah. The victorious Quraysh celebrated by mutilating the bodies of the Muslims. It was reported that one of the Quraysh split open Hamzah's abdomen and cut out his liver. He took it to Hind, Abu Sufyan's wife, who ate a small part of it to avenge her father and sons who had been killed by Hamzah at Badr. The Quraysh women also reportedly made bloody necklaces from the ears and noses of the dead.

Muhammad and his companions took refuge in the rocks of Uhud. In the morning, the dead Muslims were buried in trenches, and the wounded returned to Medina. Although he was injured, Muhammad led a number of his men in pursuit of the Quraysh to deter them from further attacks against Medina. They kept their distance, lighting big fires to let the Quraysh know of their presence in hopes that the Quraysh would think they were a large army rather than just a small force. Then they returned to Medina.

Although the Muslims had greater losses than the Quraysh, Abu Sufyan had not succeeded in removing Muhammad from Medina, and so the battle essentially was a draw with neither side claiming a decisive victory. The battle was, however, a spiritual defeat for Muhammad and his followers because they had believed that

## CHANGES IN THE RULES OF MARRIAGE

*Because the large number of casualties as a result of the battle of Uhud resulted in many orphans and widows, it became necessary to create new regulations to provide for them. The women and children needed protection. Shortly after the battle of Uhud, Muhammad received a revelation that dealt with the problem. The revelation appears in Sura 4, Verse 3 of the Koran.*

*"If you are afraid that you will treat the orphans unjustly, then marry what women seem good to you, twos and threes and fours; if you are afraid you will not deal equitably, then one."*

*Author Karen Armstrong writes:*

There was probably a shortage of men in Arabia, which left a surplus of unmarried women who were often badly exploited. The Qur'an is most concerned about this problem and resorted to polygamy as a way of dealing with it. This would enable all the girls who had been orphaned to be married, but it insisted that a man could take more than one wife only if he promised to administer their property equitably. It also stipulates that no orphan girl should be married to her guardian against her will, as if she were moveable property. The Qur'an also makes a provision for divorce. . . . In Arabia it was customary for a man to give a *mahl*, a dowry to his bride. This had usually been absorbed by the woman's male relatives, but in Islam the dowry was to be given directly to the woman herself. To this day, women are allowed to do whatever they choose with this money: give it to charity, build a swimming pool or start a business. But in the event of a divorce, a man is not allowed to reclaim the *mahl*, so a woman's security is assured.

they were unbeatable and fought with the protection of Allah. Now, many questioned their standing in God's eyes.

## PERSECUTION OF THE JEWS CONTINUES

The Jews of Medina also noted the Muslim defeat and used it to say that Muhammad could not be accepted as Allah's prophet, since his troops suffered such great losses at Uhud. The Medinan leader Abdullah ibn Ubbayy and his followers were also critical because the defeat might have been avoided if Muhammad had followed the advice of more experienced warriors. The people who criticized Muhammad began to be called by the Muslims "The Doubters" or "The Hypocrites."

The criticisms angered Muhammad, and it was not long before he took out his irritation on a second Jewish clan called the Nadir. He believed the clan was plotting to kill him, partly in retaliation for the assassination of the Jewish poet who was a member of that group. Muhammad sent the Nadir an ultimatum in which they were told they could no longer stay in Medina. When Ibn Ubbayy offered them his support, the Jews decided to resist, and they barricaded themselves inside their fortress. Ibn Ubbayy, however, had misjudged the Muslim strength and determination, and he soon withdrew his support. The Muslims then surrounded the fort so the Nadir could not leave, and at the end of two weeks, they began chopping down the palm trees that surrounded the fortress. Seeing that defeat

was certain, the Nadir surrendered, begging for their lives. Muhammad ordered that they immediately leave Medina carrying only the possessions that they could load onto their camels.

Although they were defeated, the Nadir left Medina in a proud procession with the women, dressed in their jewels and finest clothes, beating tambourines and playing music. Some of them went to Syria, but many settled in Khaybar, a Jewish settlement to the north from which they aided the Quraysh in building up resistance to the Muslims among the tribes of the region. The tension between the Muslims and the Quraysh continued.

## THE AFFAIR OF THE LIE

During 626 and 627, Muhammad continued making raids against tribes that he thought might form alliances with the Quraysh. In December 627 he set out on an expedition against a small tribe that had always been loyal to Mecca because he believed that the chief was preparing an attack on Medina. Attacking the tribe by surprise, his troops took everyone captive and thoroughly looted the tribe's possessions. During the peace negotiations, the daughter of the chief was given to Muhammad as a mistress. When she later became a Muslim, he married her.

So that he would have company, one or more of the wives usually accompanied Muhammad on his expeditions. On one of the trips, Aisha, Muhammad's favorite wife, discovered that she had lost her necklace in the sand outside the camp and

*The wives of Muhammad (lower left) cover their faces with veils after the affair of the lie.*

went back to look for it. Because she traveled in a closed compartment mounted on her camel, her absence was not noticed, and the group left without her. When Aisha returned and discovered that the caravan was gone, she wrapped herself in her cloak, knowing that someone would return for her. While she was waiting, one of the soldiers who had dropped behind the rest of the group came upon her. He offered to let her ride his camel to the group that had gone ahead. The next morning when they reached the army's camp, the Hypocrites began to spread the rumor that Aisha and the soldier were involved in an improper relationship. The scandal spread throughout the camp.

Ibn Ubbayy and his followers took the opportunity to weaken Muhammad's position and accused her of adultery. Muhammad himself was unsure of her innocence. The scandal grew for weeks and was on the verge of causing a serious disagreement among the Muslims, because Abu Bakr, Aisha's father and Muhammad's chief lieutenant, might lose his power if the story was proven to be true. Finally, when sufficient time had passed to prove that Aisha had not become pregnant, Muhammad decided the question in her favor. Those who had accused her, including Ibn Ubbayy, lost influence, and some were beaten as punishment. The incident, known as "the affair of the lie," actually solidified Muhammad's power in Medina because it marked the end of Ibn Ubbayy's challenge to his authority.

## THE BATTLE OF THE DITCH

While Muhammad was consolidating his authority in Medina, his opponents in Mecca were assembling a large force that included men from the various nomadic tribes. They were helped by the expelled Jewish clans who wanted to defeat Muhammad and reclaim their lands. It is believed that this force numbered between seventy-five hundred and ten thousand men, divided into three separate groups. On March 31, 627, this force set out toward Medina and set up camp nearby.

Muhammad and the Muslims were worried because they had about three thousand fighters. Because they were outnumbered, Muhammad made a tactical

*Muhammad's opponents, including expelled Jewish tribes, set up camp outside Medina (pictured).*

decision to fortify Medina by digging a deep trench, called the *Khandaq*, in the places most vulnerable to attack by fighters on horseback. Because Medina was surrounded by lava flows on three sides, the trench was dug on the north side of the oasis. Everyone, even children, helped dig the trench, and in six days it was completed. As the enemy approached, the women and children were taken to fortifications within Medina, and Muhammad took up his position in a command post on a nearby hill called Mount Sal'.

The enemy set up two camps to the north and the northwest. When they tried to attack, they were surprised to find the trench. On the other side, the Muslim archers were massed and ready for the attack. Whenever a horseman tried to cross the trench, he was bombarded with arrows. The few who succeeded in leaping over the ditch were driven back.

When they saw that their greater numbers would not guarantee them an easy victory, the Quraysh's morale began to fall. Food was scarce for both sides, and the cold weather was unusually harsh. After several weeks the Quraysh coalition began to break up, and some began to leave. The Quraysh, in spite of their greater force, had failed to remove Muhammad's threat to their power and prosperity.

For Muhammad, this was a great victory with few casualties. The encounter proved that he could not be defeated by force. It also demonstrated his strategic skill, as his use of the trench had defeated the Quraysh even though they had more soldiers. The victory helped boost the morale of the Muslims.

## THE EXECUTION OF THE LAST JEWISH CLAN

Only one group was left that threatened Muhammad's power in Medina—a Jewish clan called the Bani Qurayzah. During the Battle of the Ditch, the Quraysh had tried to convince the clan to attack the Muslims from within Medina. Although they had not done so, they had not aided the Muslim defense. Muhammad considered this an act of treason, and he decided to take action to show his enemies that this kind of behavior would not be tolerated.

He ordered his men to meet in front of the fortifications of the Jewish community, where they set up a siege for twenty-five days. After the Jews said they would discuss terms of surrender, Muhammad assigned a man allied with the Muslims to serve as a judge and determine their fate. Although the Jews begged that they be given the same terms as the Nadir clan, this man ruled that all the men of Bani Qurayzah should be put to death and the women and children sold into slavery. The following day between seven hundred and nine hundred men were beheaded in the marketplace, and the women and children were sold. Muhammad took Rayhana, a Jewish woman widowed by the massacre, as a mistress. After she later converted to Islam, he married her.

Although Muhammad's action against the Jews was brutal, scholars argue that it was consistent with the accepted behavior of the time when an enemy had no rights. When he first arrived in Medina, Muhammad had hoped to make the Jews into allies, but when they challenged his authority and allied themselves with the Quraysh, they became his enemy.

Author Karen Armstrong writes:

> The massacre of the Qurayzah is a reminder of the desperate conditions of Arabia during Muhammad's lifetime. Of course we are right to condemn it without reserve, but it was not as great a crime as it would be today. . . . All Muhammad had was the old tribal morality, which had permitted this expedient to preserve the group. The problem was compounded by the fact that Muhammad's victory had made him the most powerful chief in Arabia at the head of a group that was not a conventional tribe. He had just begun to transcend tribalism and was in a no man's land between two stages of social development.[29]

Muhammad's actions were brutal, but they consolidated his power and discouraged his enemies from further conspiracies. A small number of Jews did remain in Medina after the massacre, but these were not hostile to Islam.

In the five years that Muhammad had lived in Medina, he had risen from an exile who had been forced to flee from his home and clan in Mecca to the most powerful leader in his new community. He had eliminated any opposition that threatened his personal authority and the dominance of Islam. He had also proved himself as a military leader. By 627 the Muslims controlled all aspects of life in Medina and were ready to look outward to greater conquests.

# 6 The Return to Mecca

Muhammad's victory over the Quraysh during the siege at Medina was proof that his moral and political strength had grown. His goals of uniting all Arabs across tribal affiliations, expanding Muslim political control throughout the Arabian peninsula, and bringing the religious message that Allah was the one, all-powerful god to as many people as possible were becoming a reality. He was not yet ready to openly attack Mecca, but he continued to try to weaken the Quraysh's monopoly on trade.

Throughout 627 and 628 Muhammad continued to forge new alliances with neighboring tribes. Those tribes that still supported the Quraysh became targets of Muslim raids in retaliation. He also sent Muslim expeditions to the north to make converts and to attract some of the Syrian trade. At the same time, Muhammad was developing an intelligence system of spies who informed him about what was going on in Mecca. In spite of his success he never lost his desire to ultimately return to the city of his birth.

## GOING TO MECCA

In March 628, Muhammad dreamed that he was making a pilgrimage to Mecca without opposition from the Quraysh. Believing that the dream was an omen, he made a decision that he and his followers would make a pilgrimage, called the 'umrah, to the Ka'aba. This pilgrimage was known as the lesser pilgrimage. Then, as now, there are two kinds of pilgrimages. The hajj, or greater pilgrimage, must be done on a specific day of the year, but the 'umrah can be done at any time. He invited his followers to accompany him. It was decided that they would wear the traditional white pilgrims' robes, and they were unarmed. They did decide to carry short swords for hunting. Although going to Mecca was a dangerous move, between one thousand and fourteen hundred followers decided to take the trip. They took along seventy camels, which would be sacrificed as part of the pilgrimage according to custom.

The pilgrims left Medina on March 13, 628. When the Quraysh heard that the Muslims were coming, they feared an attack and sent men on horseback to keep them away. They swore that Muhammad and his followers would not enter Mecca. To avoid the Quraysh, Muhammad found a local guide who led the Muslims to an area near Mecca called the Sanctuary

*Muhammad and followers of Islam attempted to enter the Ka'aba (pictured) in what is known as the 'umrah but were denied entrance to Mecca.*

where it was forbidden to fight. When they reached an open plain called Hudaybiyah on the edge of the protected area about eight miles from Mecca, the Muslims set up their camp and watered their camels.

Scouts sent by the Quraysh to determine Muhammad's intentions returned to Mecca, reporting that the Muslims were dressed as pilgrims and that their camels were adorned with garlands, which meant they had been prepared for sacrifice. The Quraysh then sent a trusted representative to tell Muhammad that they were determined to fight and would never allow the Muslims to enter Mecca. The Muslims replied that they would never abandon the prophet.

A short time later, Muhammad sent his son-in-law Uthman ibn Affan to Mecca to negotiate with the Quraysh. It was believed that the Quraysh would not harm him because he was second cousin of the Quraysh leader Abu Sufyan. Although the Quraysh listened to him, they were unimpressed by his arguments and decided to detain him as a hostage. Meanwhile, a rumor that Uthman had been killed reached the Muslims. It was believed that the Quraysh would stop at nothing if they had killed a man whose life should have been protected by tribal loyalties.

Muhammad was so upset by the bad news that he declared that he would not leave without facing the Quraysh. At this time it seemed that the pilgrimage was about to disintegrate into warfare. It was a moment of crisis that could have resulted in a serious defeat for the Muslims, but the Quraysh did not take advantage of this opportunity to attack. Author Sir John Glubb writes:

> The Meccans had at this moment their last opportunity to destroy Islam and Muhammad for once and for all. The [prophet's] idea of a pilgrimage had placed him at the mercy of his enemies . . . with only a small force, armed with nothing but swords. If the Quraysh had been led by a single, determined commander, they could have seized this priceless opportunity to end the struggle in a few hours. But, as had been proved after Uhud, the Quraysh leaders were incapable of swift, determined action.[30]

It is reported that Muhammad then went into a period of intense concentration in which he searched for a solution to fighting a battle he would probably lose. Believing he could be attacked at any moment, he then called his followers to affirm their loyalty to him and his cause. One by one, they walked past him to pledge their faith in Islam and their readiness to fight. Historically, this event is known as the *bay'at al-ridwan*, or the Pledge of Good Pleasure. Shortly after

everyone had taken the oath, the good news came from Mecca that Uthman was not dead.

## THE TREATY OF HUDAYBIYAH

When Muhammad saw a small group of Meccans approaching his camp, he realized that they were coming to negotiate. After consulting with them for a long time, he accepted a treaty in which he agreed to return to Medina without visiting the Ka'aba during this visit. The treaty, however, gave the Muslims the right to return the following year at the same time to perform the lesser pilgrimage around the Ka'aba. During that time the Quraysh would leave the city for three days. The treaty also called for a ten-year truce with the condition that Muhammad promised to return any of the Quraysh who might come to Medina to convert to Islam. Any Muslim who wanted to return to Mecca and give up Islam could do so without retribution. Other tribes who wanted to make agreements with either Muhammad or the Quraysh could do so.

Muhammad's followers were very upset and confused by what appeared to be unequal terms of the agreement. The ten-year truce allowed the Quraysh to reestablish their prosperous caravan trade but prohibited the Muslims from making raids on them, resulting in a loss of revenue. They were also uncomfortable with the agreement that any Quraysh who converted to Islam would have to be returned to Mecca, while the Quraysh did not have to return Muslim defectors to Medina. It

*One by one, Muslims affirm their loyalty to Muhammad and pledge their faith to Islam during the* bay'at al-ridwan.

appeared that Muhammad had abandoned the struggle to spread the message of Islam and was giving an advantage to the Quraysh. Many followers voiced their disagreement, and some wanted to rebel.

As soon as the Quraysh left, Muhammad calmed his followers down somewhat by announcing that since they could not enter Mecca, they would now observe the rites of the lesser pilgrimage at Hudaybiyah. Every man was to shave his head, and the sacrificial camels would be killed. When his followers still seemed hostile, he sacrificed his own camel to appease them. This action, which was a familiar part of the pilgrimage, broke the

followers' depression, and soon they all performed the ritual sacrifice. They then all shaved their hair and completed the ceremonies of the *'umrah.* For the followers, these rituals reinforced the awareness that Islam, while stressing the belief in one god, also incorporated the traditions of the ancient Arab religion.

On the way back to Medina, Muhammad had a revelation which is called in the Koran the Sura of Victory. The revelation states that a great victory had been achieved at Hudaybiyah. It acknowledges that the Muslims had committed acts of faith when they decided to take the pilgrimage and when they swore loyalty to

Muhammad. Also, the negotiations with the Quraysh had given public recognition to Muhammad's position and power. Although some of the terms of the Treaty of Hudaybiyah seemed difficult, the agreement had been a victory for the long term.

Author Karen Armstrong writes, "Muhammad could see further than anybody else at Hudaybiyah; even though the pilgrimage had not turned out as he expected, it had been an inspiration that put him on the road to peace."[31]

## MUHAMMAD'S WIVES

In seventh-century Arabia, marriages were arranged, and women had very little choice in the matter. Men were permitted to have up to four wives. Taking multiple wives was a way for the widows of the men killed in raids and battles to be protected. Marriages were also a way to form political alliances. In a revelation that he received after the battle at Uhud, Muhammad was granted permission to have more than four wives, a right that was given only to him and not to his followers.

Although he had been monogamous during his marriage to his first wife, Khadijah, after her death he had eleven more wives. Of these all were widows except for Aisha, the youngest wife. Some were said to be very beautiful, and others such as Sawdah were considered unattractive. His marriages to most of these later wives also were political alliances with his close associates. Several of the wives were Jewish women who belonged to clans that he defeated; however, he did not marry them until they converted to Islam. Although he had six children (two sons died in infancy) during his marriage to Khadijah, none of the later wives produced children during their marriages with Muhammad. In his sixties, he did have a son with his Egyptian concubine, but that child also died in infancy.

Muhammad had a room built off the courtyard of his house for each wife. Because many of his wives were young women, he was concerned that they might attract the attention of other men. After he received a revelation called "The Verses of the Curtain," he ruled that his wives should be separated from the rest of the community by a curtain. This was to prevent his enemies from spreading rumors that could damage his prestige. For Muhammad's wives, covering their faces became a symbol of their status. Later, this rule was extended to requiring women to cover their faces with their veils whenever they went out. Before this time, Arabian women did not wear veils.

In his book *The Life and Times of Muhammad*, Sir John Glubb writes: "[Muhammad] enjoyed the company of women. He considered it an innocent pleasure for which he praised God. He was always kind and considerate towards his wives, who gave him this enjoyment."

After Muhammad's death, his wives played an important role in the development of Islam, and they were frequently asked about his opinions and ideas.

## The Conquest of Khaybar, September 628

Muhammad knew that in order to calm the men who were dissatisfied with the Treaty of Hudaybiyah, he would have to take decisive action; so a short time after the Muslims had returned to Medina, he announced his desire to attack the oasis of Khaybar located seventy-five miles to the north. There were several reasons for the aggressive act. The first was defense. Khaybar was a largely Jewish settlement which included members of the Nadir tribe that Muhammad had exiled from Medina several years earlier. Muhammad wanted to remove any threat these groups might pose to the security of Medina. A second reason was psychological. Muhammad wanted to remove any lingering bitterness that his followers might pose to the terms agreed upon at Hudaybiyah. Engaging in an expedition that promised rich spoils to the victors was a way to refocus their energy. For this reason, only those who had made the recent pilgrimage were allowed to participate in the raid that took place in September 628.

Khaybar was a strong settlement surrounded by a number of castles or forts located on the tops of hills. Many thought that it would be impossible for Muhammad's force of around six hundred men to conquer the community. The tribes of Khaybar, however, did not cooperate with one another and could not organize a united defense. Muhammad's approach was to lay siege to the oasis and attack the strongholds one by one, attacking with volleys of arrows until his troops could enter and claim victory. After several of the forts had surrendered, the Nadir offered terms of surrender, which Muhammad accepted. In return for half their date crop, Muhammad offered Khaybar military protection. The dates would be divided between those Muslims who had taken part in the expedition, with Muhammad receiving one-fifth of what had been captured.

The battle had several personal consequences for Muhammad. Shortly after the agreement, a Jewish woman named Zaynab invited him and several of his companions to dinner. Although she seemed friendly, she planned to poison the Muslims in retaliation for the deaths of her father, uncle, and husband in the battle. When she prepared one of Muhammad's favorite foods, roast lamb, she inserted poison into the shoulder. At his first bite, Muhammad noticed that the food tasted strange, and he spit it out, but one of his companions ate the meat and soon died. When Muhammad questioned her, Zaynab admitted to poisoning the food. Rather than treating her harshly, he forgave her for her treachery. Scholars cannot explain why he was so forgiving on this occasion. Perhaps one explanation is that Muhammad's treatment of women was usually kind. In a later instance, he forgave Hind, the wife of the Quraysh leader Abu Sufyan, for her hostility against the Muslims during the battle of Uhud, and permitted her to become a Muslim.

The victory at Khaybar also brought Muhammad another wife, a beautiful seventeen-year-old Jewish woman named Safiyah who was the widow of one of the warriors who had fought against the Muslims. She agreed to become a Muslim, and the marriage soon took place in a tent in the oasis near Khaybar.

After the victory at Khaybar, other Jewish colonies nearby also submitted to similar terms and were allowed to keep their property if they paid a tax to the Muslims. Although a number of Jewish families still lived in Medina and elsewhere in Arabia, the battle of Khaybar ended their political power in Arabia during the remainder of Muhammad's lifetime.

## THE RETURN TO MEDINA

When the Muslims returned to Medina, Muhammad was greeted by the group of Muslims who had thirteen years earlier emigrated to Abyssinia (he had earlier written to Abyssinia to ask them to return to Arabia). Among the group was his cousin Jafar and a widow, Umm Habiba, who was also the daughter of the Quraysh leader Abu Sufyan. Earlier, a marriage had been arranged between Muhammad and the widow, and quarters had been

---

### AISHA

Of all Muhammad's later wives, the youngest, Aisha, was his favorite. It is believed that she was born in Mecca in 615 to one of the earliest Muslim families. Her parents were Abu Bakr and Um Ruman, early followers of Muhammad. Aisha had a special place among Muhammad's wives because with her he was able to relax. It is reported that she was highly intelligent. After her marriage to Muhammad when she was nine, she would listen to his lectures, asking questions about issues about which she was unclear. When Muhammad left Medina on trips, he told his followers to consult with Aisha if they had any religious questions.

Muhammad tried to be an impartial husband. He spent a night with each wife in turn and had them draw lots to determine which ones would accompany him on his expeditions. Still, the other wives complained that he favored Aisha. His answer was that she was the only one of his living wives in whose company he received revelations.

Aisha also played the most significant role in the years following Muhammad's death. Because she had been present when Muhammad received many of the revelations, she was able to help interpret their meaning. It is said that she knew the entire Koran by memory. Because of this knowledge, people sought her knowledge and interpretations, many of which became part of the traditions that relate incidents in Muhammad's life. She also played a role in the violent politics that took place after Muhammad died. She led a revolt against Ali during the time he was caliph (A.D. 656–661). She died around 681 at the age of sixty-five.

prepared for her near the mosque. The marriage was a political move aimed at improving relationships between Muhammad and the Quraysh.

By this time Muhammad had been married eleven times. Ten of the wives were still alive. Muhammad's new marriages caused a disagreement in the harem, as Aisha, Muhammad's youngest and favorite wife, was very upset with the arrival of more wives. Umm Habibah, who was older, was not a threat, but the beautiful Safiyah was not welcomed. At first, she was teased and ridiculed by the other wives, but as time went on she became friends with Aisha and Hafsah, the two other young wives.

## A RETURN TO MECCA

A year after the truce at Hudaybiyah, Muhammad and his followers again set out to make the lesser pilgrimage to Mecca as had been agreed upon in the treaty. Historians believe that between fifteen hundred and two thousand followers made the trip.

As the Muslims approached the Sanctuary, the Quraysh left the city for three days as was agreed and gathered on the surrounding mountains to watch what was happening in the valley below. In the morning the procession of Muslims arrived with Muhammad at the lead riding on Qaswa, his camel, and surrounded by his closest lieutenants Umar, Ali, and Abu Bakr. The

Muslims had also brought sixty camels to be sacrificed. Muhammad's first stop was at the Ka'aba where he kissed the black stone and circled the monument seven times, followed by the other pilgrims.

The lesser pilgrimage also involved running back and forth seven times between two low hills called Mawra and Safa. Muhammad incorporated these pagan rites into Islam in order to show that the new religion had its roots in the most sacred traditions of the Arab people. These rituals are still practiced today during the *hajj*.

During the three-day pilgrimage, Muhammad's uncle 'Abbas, who had remained in Mecca, visited him and offered him as a wife his sister, Maymunah, who was a twenty-seven-year-old widow. 'Abbas also finally agreed to become a Muslim. Muhammad accepted the offer of another wife and invited the Quraysh to come to the wedding. They rejected this invitation and told the Muslims that they must leave the city at the end of the three days. As this was according to the terms of the Treaty of Hudabiyah, Muhammad agreed to do so, and the pilgrims returned to Medina.

The lesser pilgrimage to Mecca in 629 was a great accomplishment that was discussed throughout Arabia. The Quraysh observed the discipline of the Muslims who peacefully entered the city for three days. The pilgrimage was also an important step toward spreading Islam throughout the Arabian peninsula.

# 7 The Final Years

During the last three years of Muhammad's life, he sought to spread the message of Islam to even more people by widening his operations to other parts of Arabia and to neighboring countries such as Yemen. His goal was to increase his strength and create an Islamic political power. By this time, his military power was acknowledged to be great, but he preferred using diplomacy to armed force whenever possible. After the three-day pilgrimage to Mecca, his popularity increased among his followers who loved and respected him. Part of his appeal was that he was approachable and considered himself one with his people. It was not unusual to see him seated on the ground in the mosque, and he frequently walked among the people, picking up children and hugging them.

## NEW CONVERTS

One of the important consequences following the Muslims' three-day pilgrimage to Mecca was that a number of the most prominent young Quraysh men converted to Islam. They felt that Muhammad's power was greater than that of the Meccan leaders, and they wanted to be on the winning side.

One of the most significant conversions was that of Khalid ibn al-Walid, an important Quraysh warrior who had fought against the Muslims. His arrival in Medina and his subsequent conversion was a cause for celebration among the Muslims. He had been a leading officer at the battle of Uhud and the siege of Medina and was responsible for slaying many Muslims. According to the rules of the tribal system, the families of those he had killed could seek retribution, but Muhammad assured him that by becoming a Muslim, he had eliminated any retaliations for these deaths. His acceptance of Islam overrode tribal affiliations. Khalid's military experience would be an asset in future forays.

## JOYS AND SORROWS

Although Muhammad had enjoyed great success with the pilgrimage to Mecca, the year 629 was not without its personal sorrows. Shortly after his return to Medina, his oldest daughter, Zaynab, died. Biographer Martin Lings describes the funeral:

## TREATMENT OF ANIMALS

Before Islam many Arabians were quite cruel to animals. They would cut off lumps of flesh to eat while the animal was still alive, and animal fights were a popular sport. During his lifetime, Muhammad tried to teach Muslims to respect the natural world, both through revelations and by example. According to a story in the *Hadith,* as his army marched to Mecca to conquer it, he saw a female dog with her puppies. Muhammad gave orders that the dogs should not be disturbed. He then posted a guard to make sure that his orders were obeyed. He stated, "Verily, there is a heavenly reward for every act of kindness done to living animals."

He also prohibited cutting horses' manes and tails and keeping them saddled for long periods of time. Branding animals at any soft spot where they might be in pain was also forbidden, as were organized animal fights. However, the custom of sacrificing camels or other animals at the end of a pilgrimage continued to be practiced then as it is today. It is said that this symbolizes the willingness of the prophet Abraham to sacrifice his son if God commanded it.

"When the ablutions had been performed, the Prophet took off an undergarment he was wearing, and told them to wrap her in it before they shrouded her. Then he led the funeral prayer, and prayed also beside her grave."[32]

Not long after Zaynab's death, however, Muhammad found out that Maryam, a Christian Egyptian slave who had been given to him as a mistress by the ruler of Egypt, was pregnant. Although he sired six children with Khadijah, none of his later wives had become pregnant. He loved and respected Maryam, but he had not married her because she was not a Muslim. When the baby, a boy named Ibrahim, was born the following year, there was much rejoicing. The baby received special care, and every other day sheep's milk was specially delivered for him. Muhammad, whose two sons with Khadijah had died in early childhood, was delighted to have a son, and he loved carrying the baby around Medina. Muhammad's household brought him much happiness and was a source of stability in his life at a time when he was also encouraging the greater expansion of Islam.

## THE BATTLE OF MOTA

During the latter part of his life, Muhammad turned his attention to conquering the north. Much of this area was under the control of the Byzantine Empire, which had separated from the Roman Empire in 395. By 629, the empire controlled the lands to the north and east of Arabia including Syria, Palestine, and Egypt. In

September 629 the Muslims had their first battle against a force outside the Arab world. The details surrounding the causes of this battle have not been preserved, but it is known that the force was led by Muhammad's adopted son Zayd, Ali's brother Jafar, and a Muslim from Medina named 'Abd Allah ibn Rawahah. Muhammad accompanied the troops for the first day, and then returned to Medina.

When the Muslims arrived at the Syrian border, they received information that a huge army of tribesmen and imperial Byzantine troops was waiting to attack. At first, the Muslims voted to advance, but when Zayd saw the combined forces of the tribesmen and the Byzantine troops, he ordered a retreat to Mota, a nearby village located on an open plain.

As commander, it was Zayd's responsibility to lead the charge. Waving the white war flag that Muhammad had given him, he attacked and was soon killed, as was Jafar. Biographer Sir John Glubb describes the combat: "Jafar . . . was close behind and, snatching up the banner, raised it once more crying, 'Paradise, O Muslims, Paradise.' The enemy closed in round the heroic Jafar. Tradition relates that when both his hands were cut off holding the staff of the banner, he still kept it erect by clasping it between his two stumps until he also, covered with wounds, received a mortal thrust from a Byzantine soldier."[33]

Khalid, the experienced Quraysh warrior who had led the Meccan forces at Uhud, then took control and ordered a retreat. Although the battle had been bloody, casualties were few. Some accounts say sixteen Muslims had been killed; the historian Ibn Ishaq reports eight.

When the troops finally returned to Medina, people threw dirt at them saying they were cowards who had run away in the face of battle. Muhammad had to intervene to defend them saying, "Nay, they are not runaways, but returners again to the fight, if God will."[34]

The loss of Zayd and Jafar deeply affected Muhammad. He went to their homes to console their wives and children and ordered food to be prepared for them for the next few days. The defeat at Mota encouraged some of the northern tribes to continue to resist the advance of Islam, but by 630 the Muslims had strengthened their position, extending their influence to tribes on all sides of Medina. Although some of this dominance was political, a large part of it was caused by the spiritual appeal of Islam.

## THE FALL OF MECCA

For Muhammad, control of Mecca was essential for the expansion of Islam, but he was bound to a ten-year truce with the Quraysh by the Treaty of Hudabiyah, which meant that he could not make the first move to attack. In November 629, however, the truce was broken when a Bedouin tribe allied with the Quraysh attacked a tribe under the protection of the Muslims, killing twenty people. The Quraysh knew that Muhammad would probably seek revenge, so they sent the leader, Abu Sufyan, to Medina to confer with him to seek a solution to avoid a

*Outnumbered by tribesmen and Byzantine troops, Zayd's Muslim army perishes at Mota.*

violent confrontation and all-out fighting in Mecca. Scholars are unsure what compromises Abu Sufyan and Muhammad actually agreed to, but after a short time in Medina, Abu Sufyan returned to Mecca and helped to pave the way for the Quraysh to surrender to Muhammad's forces. He told the Quraysh that the city would not be in danger if the Meccans welcomed Muhammad without resistance. If people remained in their homes, they would not be harmed.

Although Abu Sufyan had led the Quraysh forces against the Muslims at Uhud, he now believed that the best course was to reach an understanding with Muhammad and to perhaps convert to Islam. He was a practical man who had changed his opinion of Islam after seeing Muhammad's victories and the discipline of the Muslims on the battlefield and during the pilgrimage to Mecca. His own daughter, Umm Habiba, had converted to Islam and had become one of Muhammad's wives the previous year.

Not long after Abu Sufyan departed from Medina, Muhammad began gathering a huge force of ten thousand men to march on Mecca. The troops set out on January 1, 630. At the outskirts of Mecca, he divided his troops into four groups and ordered that no force was to be used except in self-defense. There was a short list of persons who, if caught, were to be immediately executed. These included people who had insulted Islam and those who had become Muslims and had later rejected the religion.

## THE IDOLS ARE SMASHED

Muhammad pitched his tent on a hill to the northwest of town and watched his troops occupy Mecca. Only one small force attacked the Muslims, but they were easily subdued. Then, mounting his camel, Muhammad entered Mecca and rode around the Ka'aba seven times, touching the black stone with his stick each time he passed, calling "Allahu akbar!" ("Allah is great!") His next order was for his troops to smash the 360 idols that stood near the Ka'aba and burn their remains. He also ordered the destruction of murals depicting the pagan gods that adorned the interior of the Ka'aba.

Muhammad stayed in Mecca for two weeks. During this time, no one was forced to convert to Islam. Muhammad's purpose was not to punish the Quraysh but rather to come to an agreement with them. He thought it would be more important if the people came to Islam on their own terms instead of being forced into it. The author Maxime Rodinson explains: "Like his later successors on a worldwide scale, Muhammad had the sense to create a favorable climate for the adoption of his religion and then to leave matters to take their own course without hurrying them. Conversion carried with it considerable advantages. . . . Social pressures no longer worked in the favor of paganism but favored Islam instead. It was enough; in a few years, paganism in Mecca was a thing of the past."[35]

## GROWING FAME

The peaceful conquest of Mecca was a great victory for Muhammad, and his authority and prestige grew. His followers treated him with reverence and ultimate adoration. When his hair was cut, people collected the hair as a sacred relic, and when he washed, they drank the dirty water. Even the shavings from his fingernails were considered holy. In spite of his growing fame, however, he did not want to be treated formally, saying he was a man like any other. He refused to wear jewels or expensive clothing, and often he was found sitting on the ground in the mosque in the company of the poorest people in Medina.

However, not long after the conquest, a group of nomadic tribes gathered at Taif,

*On January 1, 630, Muhammad assembles a large army outside of Mecca (pictured) and prepares to take the city.*

the agricultural town to the east of Mecca, to attack the Muslims and challenge his authority. Although Muhammad's forces were greatly outnumbered, they conquered the tribes in January 630. Muhammad gave the largest part of the wealth that had been taken in the battle to Abu Sufyan and the other Quraysh who had helped, and as a result, many converted to Islam. The Muslims from Medina were upset because they feared that Muhammad was turning his back on them and was favoring the men from his birthplace. Very diplomatically, he expressed his deep gratitude for the assistance he had received from the Medinans and assured

them that Medina would always be his home.

When he returned to Medina, Muhammad's prestige grew even greater. Tribes from around Arabia began to send delegations to Medina to pledge their allegiance to the Muslims. Conversion to Islam was relatively easy. They had to promise to destroy their idols and worship Allah. They also had to agree not to attack the Muslims and to pay a tax for the poor called *zakat*. The *zakat*, or giving to the needy, is still one of the basic requirements for followers of Islam. The Islamic community was well on its way to becoming a confederation of tribes.

Although Muhammad's power was well acknowledged as a politician, his family life was becoming turbulent.

## TROUBLE IN THE HAREM

Muhammad, who had always lived simply, became concerned about the effect his growing prosperity was having on his harem, the women of his household. The wives argued about how the new possessions should be divided among them. One disagreement, probably over the division of some of the recently obtained spoils acquired in one of the raids, caused him to leave his wives for one month, during which time he retired to a small, poorly furnished room on the roof of the mosque. Muhammad's absence became a serious situation because the disunity in his household threatened not only his marriages, but also the political alliances with his allies and friends who were related to his wives. To resolve the situation, he gave the wives two alternatives called the "Verses of Choice" in the Koran. They could choose divorce or they could agree to live a simple life according to the rules of Islam. The wives decided to agree to his terms. At this time it was also ordered that the wives could not remarry after Muhammad's death because the future marriages might create dynasties that would create dissension among the Muslims.

Of the ten wives in his harem at this time, Aisha was his favorite. In later *hadiths*, she related that Muhammad helped the wives with their household chores.

### THE FIVE PILLARS OF FAITH

*Because Muhammad believed that salvation was earned through living a virtuous life, Islam emphasizes faith and behavior. While Islam does not stress ritual, the practice of the religion requires followers to follow five duties called "The Five Pillars."*

*Author Emory C. Bogle describes these in his book* Islam: Origin and Belief:

Even the most individualistic Muslims must practice their religion within the framework of five obligatory duties, which are commonly called the Five Pillars of Islam. Reliable *hadith* quote the Prophet Muhammad as saying, "Islam has been built upon five things." Accordingly, all Muslims are expected to (1) profess their faith (*shahadah*) at all times; (2) perform five daily prayers (*salat*); (3) annually contribute alms (*zakat*); (4) annually perform a thirty-day fast (*siyam*); and (5) make at least one pilgrimage (*hajj*) to Mecca during the believer's lifetime. Muslims could meet the minimal demands of all these duties except the *hajj* with a modest effort.

# Ali

The loss of his infant son by Khadijah was a source of sorrow for Muhammad. This loss was somewhat softened when he adopted Ali, the five-year-old son of his uncle Abu Talib who was having financial troubles during a year of severe famine. When Ali was around ten years old, he became one of the first Muslims.

In Medina, when Muhammad's youngest daughter Fatimah was twenty, he decided that she should marry Ali, who had grown up with her as a brother. Because Ali did not have an inheritance from Abu Talib, he was hesitant to enter into the marriage, but Muhammad urged him to do so. At first the young couple were very poor and struggled to survive. He and his family continued to live simple lives throughout his lifetime, even after he became the fourth caliph.

Ali is said to have fought in nearly all the major battles of Islam with distinction, and at the battle of Uhud he received more than sixteen wounds. He was also a scholar of Arabic literature, and was known for his sermons, speeches, and letters.

In the struggle for power that occurred after Muhammad's death, a group of Muslims supported Ali as leader of the community, but a majority backed Abu Bakr, who became the first caliph. Ali's claim to leadership was that he was the closest adult male descendant of Muhammad, and his children who were Muhammad's grandchildren were the only direct descendants.

In 656, Ali became the fourth caliph, or leader of the Muslims. His rule was based on the concept that a Muslim ruler must not be separated from his people, but should live by the principles set forth by Muhammad. His followers were called the *Shiah-iAli*, or the party of Ali. This group believes that Muslims should be led by a direct descendant of Muhammad. Today, the followers of this group are known as Shiites. In 662 Ali was assassinated in the mosque while he was praying. His assassin, who was from a splinter group, stabbed him with a poisoned sword.

This was unusual behavior for the time, but Muhammad wanted to encourage Muslims to be more considerate to women. Aisha was able to tease Muhammad, and with her he was able to relax a bit. The two would often wash in the same bowl and drink from the same cup, and it is told that she enjoyed putting perfume in his hair. She was the only one of the wives that he declared to love. Aisha was very intelligent, and after Muhammad's death she would become a respected authority on his life and the religious practices of Islam.

In 630 (some scholars say 632), Muhammad again experienced sorrow when his baby son Ibrahim died at the age of seventeen or eighteen months. The child had started to walk and was beginning to talk when he became ill. It was soon clear that he would not survive his illness, and he died in Muhammad's arms. As Muhammad may have hoped that his son would succeed him as leader of the Muslims, the baby's death was a great blow.

During an expedition to Tabuk near the border of the Byzantine Empire, Umm Kulthum, one of his daughters by Khadijah, also died. His only remaining biological child was his daughter Fatimah, who was married to his ward Ali. Muhammad was devoted to their two sons, Hasan and Husayn, and he let them climb on his back and pretend he was a horse.

## A WARNING TO THE PAGANS

When the first pilgrimage season after the Muslim occupation of Mecca came around in 631, Muhammad, who now was sixty, decided to remain in Medina. He delegated the leadership of the pilgrimage to Abu Bakr. Not long after the pilgrims' departure, he had a revelation that he felt was important to share with the assembled Muslims and pagans celebrating the annual rites. In the message, Muhammad declared a four-month grace period for all pagans. After that time, any who had not converted to Islam could be attacked or killed. The wording of the ruling was harsh. "So when the forbidden months [the grace period] are passed, kill the polytheists where ever you find them. Seize them, lay siege to them, and lay ambushes for them. But if they repent and say their prayers and pay the poor tax,

release them and set them free."[36] This ruling applied only to pagans and exempted Christians and Jews, who were not to be persecuted because they, too, worshiped one god. He also stated that in the future, only Muslims would be permitted to make the pilgrimage to Mecca. The area around the Ka'aba was to be considered holy and off-limits to non-Muslims. Later, the early Muslims extended the holy area to include the rest of Mecca and Medina. These new rules brought more converts into the Muslim camp.

When the tribes who had not yet converted to Islam heard that the Muslims were declaring war against the pagans, many decided it was time for them to also convert. In 631 delegations from all over Arabia arrived in Medina to make peace with Muhammad. The year is called "the Year of Deputations." Conversion was simple. All a person had to do was repeat the statement of faith, "There is no god but God, and Muhammad is his messenger," which is still the practice for converting today. The tribes then had to agree to pay a tax on their lands and livestock in order to join the Muslim community. They were also obligated to attack neighboring tribes who still practiced the pagan religion. Muhammad scored a diplomatic coup when a group of Yemeni chiefs converted to Islam and then returned to Yemen to attack the remaining polytheistic tribes, bringing that area under Islam without his having to send an army there. The converts in Yemen were taught the rituals of Islam and were told that future disputes were to be settled by Islamic law rather than tribal customs. Islam was

*The angel Gabriel visits Muhammad, which inspires him to introduce Arabians to Islam.*

becoming a way of life that controlled the daily actions of Muslims.

## MUHAMMAD'S LAST PILGRIMAGE TO MECCA—632

In February 632 Muhammad announced that he would lead the great pilgrimage, or *hajj*, to Mecca. Over thirty thousand

worshipers joined him. The trip from Medina to Mecca took ten days, arriving on March 3. After he entered the city, he went to the Ka'aba, circling the site the required seven times. He also visited other places in the vicinity of Mecca. On the ninth day of the pilgrimage, he preached a sermon at Mount Arafat, a large granite hill about forty miles east of Mecca. The mosque of Namira was later built on the site, where it is thought that Muhammad preached the sermon that stressed the brotherhood of all Muslims. The sermon is still read today as part of the pilgrimage to Mecca.

By now, the pilgrimage was a purely Muslim rite, as non-Muslims were forbidden to enter the city. Although the ceremonies and rituals were very similar to those that had been practiced in pagan times, Muhammad gave them new meaning and importance, which ensured a continuity between the past and the present. The rituals reminded Muslims that they had dedicated themselves to Allah. The observances of Muhammad's final trip to Mecca were incorporated into the traditions that are still practiced by Muslims who make the *hajj* to Mecca.

## MUHAMMAD'S LAST DAYS

When Muhammad returned to Medina at the end of March, he was in ill health, but in spite of his weakness and painful headaches, he continued to lead the daily prayers. To ease the pain, he would wrap a cloth around his head. At the beginning of June his condition worsened, and he moved into the rooms of his favorite wife, Aisha. In view of his ill health, Abu Bakr replaced him in leading the daily prayers. On the last day of his life, however, when he made an appearance in the courtyard and led the prayers, there was speculation that his condition was improving. When he returned to Aisha's rooms, he lay his head in her lap. She then noticed that he was losing consciousness.

The ninth-century historian al-Bukhari describes Muhammad's last moments in a *hadith* thought to be written by Aisha: "He started dipping his hand in the water and rubbing his face with it. He said 'La ilaha ill-Allah' (None has the right to be worshiped but Allah. Death has its agonies.) He then lifted his hands (towards the sky) and started saying, 'With the highest companion,' till he expired and his hand dropped down."[37]

As soon as she saw that Muhammad had died, Aisha began to mourn in the traditional Arab manner, slapping her chest and face and crying aloud.

Muhammad's death caused great confusion among the Muslims, as he had been the strong force that held the community together. Finally, Abu Bakr told the large crowd that Muhammad had dedicated himself to spreading the message that there was only one god, Allah. He said, "If there are any among you who worshiped Muhammad, he is dead. But if it is God you worshiped, He lives forever."[38]

The followers disagreed about where to bury Muhammad. Many felt that his grave should be near the graves of his three daughters and baby son and the close friends who had died before him. Others wanted to bury him in the courtyard where he preached. A solution was finally reached when Abu Bakr reminded them that Muhammad had said that a prophet should be buried where he died. It was decided to dig a grave in the floor of Aisha's room where Muhammad had spent his last hours. The place of death later was annexed to the adjacent mosque

*Muhammad delivers his last sermon shortly before his death in 632.*

and has become a site for pilgrimages for subsequent generations of Muslims.

Before the funeral all the people of Medina came to visit his body and pray, first the men followed by the women and children. Today, the Mosque of the Prophet in Medina is on the site of Muhammad's burial.

## THE MUSLIM COMMUNITY SURVIVES

After Muhammad's death the rivalry between the original inhabitants of Medina and those who had emigrated from Mecca flared up. It was finally decided that Abu Bakr, who was then elderly, would be the most acceptable as a leader for all the Arabs because he had been Muhammad's closest associate since the beginning of his mission. He was chosen as Muhammad's successor or first caliph. Soon after this decision, news came that many of the nomadic tribes had renounced Islam and refused to pay taxes. A year of civil strife followed which was more bloody than the battles that had taken place during Muhammad's lifetime. After a year, all of Arabia was under Muslim control.

## THE *HAJJ* TODAY

Every Muslim is told to make the *hajj* or pilgrimage to Mecca at least once in his or her lifetime. The *hajj* takes place during the eighth to the thirteenth day of the twelfth month of the lunar year (*Dhu al-Hajja*). The pilgrims wear the same sort of clothing, which emphasizes the equality of all before God. Emory C. Bogle describes the special dress for the *hajj* in his book *Islam: Origin and Belief*:

> Men wear two single unsewn pieces of . . . fabric (*ihram*), a costume that destroys any differentiation of rank or wealth among them. During the course of the pilgrimage, most shave their heads, which provides even greater uniformity to the assembled masses from every race and continent, and almost every nation. Although there are no prescribed garments for women, concerns for modesty require that they be fully covered except for their faces, hands, and feet. A large percentage of the women wear a white gown and scarf. Female pilgrims from societies that require veiling are permitted to perform the *hajj* unveiled.

The activities of the *hajj* follow a set pattern, which begins at the Grand Mosque. Then the pilgrims visit the Ka'aba, which is covered with a specially woven black fabric decorated with verses from the Koran in gold and white. They circle the monument seven times, going in a counterclockwise direction. The pilgrims kiss the black stone. The first night of the pilgrimage is spent at Mina, a town located about five miles from Mecca. Most camp out in a huge tent provided by the government of Saudi Arabia. The next day, they walk another ten miles to the plain of Arafat and the Mount of Mercy, where Muhammad gave his last sermon. They then collect stones, which they throw at three pillars that represent the Devil and his helpers. This symbolizes their willingness to make sacrifices for God. On the third day, they sacrifice sheep, goats, or camels. Part of the meat is eaten by the animal's owners, and the rest is given to the poor by the Saudi government. After the sacrifice, the men have their heads shaved and their nails cut. After the pilgrimage at Mecca, many pilgrims go to Medina to visit Muhammad's tomb. The *hajj* brings together people from many countries and walks of life, giving them a sense of solidarity in their faith.

With the Muslim power established in Arabia, attention turned to neighboring countries. In 633 and 634, Arabs from Medina attacked Palestine and Syria, and tribes from eastern Arabia captured part of what is now Iraq. By 637 all of Iraq was occupied by the Muslims. In 640 Egypt was invaded and by 642 was completely occupied. The same year the Persian army was destroyed, and the Persian Empire ceased to exist. Within ten years of Muhammad's death, Muslim authority extended over most of the Middle East.

## THE IMPORTANCE OF MUHAMMAD

Muhammad had lived a remarkable life and his accomplishments were many. The religion he founded was to become the basis for an empire. At the time of his death his rule extended over all of western Arabia, and he had made contact and alliances with some of the groups of eastern Arabia and Yemen. Soon after his death, the Muslims ruled most of the Middle East. As a skilled politician and mili-

*The Green Dome, as it is known to Muslims, stands above Muhammad's mausoleum.*

tary general he had been able to unify the scattered tribes into a single people who shared the same belief that there was one god. As a statesman he brought peace to the region, which was often torn by tribal wars and blood feuds.

His revelations caused a social revolution that improved the status of women, slaves, and the downtrodden of the time. Killing of unwanted babies, a common practice at the time, was banned, and the treatment of orphans and widows was reformed. Through his revelations, he established a system of law that continues to be practiced in Islamic countries. Although at times he was a complex man who committed violent acts that are difficult to understand in the setting of the contemporary world, he was also a compassionate leader who loved his followers and family.

Today, over 1 billion Muslims in the world revere Muhammad. Karen Armstrong writes, "Muhammad is . . . seen symbolically as the Perfect Man, the human archetype and image of a perfect receptivity to God. . . . Muslims seek to imitate Muhammad in their daily lives to approximate as closely as possible to this perfection and to come as close as they can to God himself."[39] Every year over 3 million people make the annual pilgrimage to worship at the Ka'aba in Mecca in much the same manner as pilgrims worshiped there in Muhammad's time. They come from every walk of life and from every continent. The religion founded by Muhammad has become a major spiritual force in the world that offers its followers meaning and guidance.

# Glossary

**Abdul Muttalib**—Muhammad's grandfather who raised him after his mother's death.

**Abu Bakr**—a wise and respected merchant of Mecca who was one of the first converts to Islam. Because he became a convert without question, many turned to him for advice, and many of these people also converted.

**Abu Jahl**—a leader of the Quraysh who hated Muhammad and his teaching.

**Abu Sufyan**—the leader of the Quraysh.

**Abu Talib**—Muhammad's uncle who raised him after his grandfather died. He was a merchant who defended Muhammad, although he never converted to Islam.

**Aisha**—Muhammad's youngest wife. She was one of a number of women he married after Khadijah died, and of these she was his favorite.

**Ali**—a son of Abu Talib who was raised by Muhammad. He was the first young man to become a Muslim.

**Aminah**—Muhammad's mother. She died when he was about six.

**Bilal**—an African slave who converted to Islam and became the first person to call the Muslims to prayer.

**Fatimah**—Muhammad's daughter by Khadijah. She was the only one who outlived her father Muhammad. She married Muhammad's cousin Ali, and they had two boys, Hasan and Husayn.

*Hadith*—traditional stories that relate incidents in Muhammad's life.

*Hajj*—the annual pilgrimage to Mecca.

**Harem**—a part of a Muslim house reserved for the residence of women. It also refers to the women in a Muslim household, including mothers, sisters, wives, mistresses, and daughters.

*Hijra*—the emigration of Muslims from Mecca to Medina.

*Jihad*—holy war against the enemies of Islam. It also refers to the struggle of an individual to overcome negative influences in his or her life.

**Ka'aba**—a cube-shaped shrine in Mecca believed to have been built by Abraham and his son Ishmael. A black stone inside the shrine is also considered holy.

**Khadijah**—Muhammad's first wife. She was the first woman to become a Muslim.

**Koran**—the holy book of Islam, which contains the revelations received by Muhammad from Allah.

**Mecca**—the city of Muhammad's birth. It is considered the holiest city of Islam and is the site of an annual pilgrimage.

**Medina**—also known as Yathrib. A town located in an oasis, which became the home of the Muslims after they were forced to leave Mecca.

**Mount Hira**—the cave where Muhammad first began receiving revelations.

**Quraysh**—a prominent Arabian tribe who opposed Muhammad's teachings. Muhammad was of the Bani Hashim branch of the Quraysh.

**Ramadan**—a holy month of fasting and prayer for Muslims.

*Salat*—the communal prayer of Islam.

*Sura*—a verse in the Koran.

*'Umrah*—the lesser pilgrimage to Mecca.

*Zakat*—giving help or money to the poor. It is one of the requirements of Islam.

**Zayd**—a slave freed and adopted by Muhammad. He became one of the first Muslims.

# Notes

## Chapter 1: The Beginning: Before the Revelations

1. Quoted in Karen Armstrong, *Muhammad: A Biography of the Prophet*. San Francisco: Harper San Francisco, 1992, p. 74.

2. Quoted in Maxime Rodinson, *Muhammad*, trans. Anne Carter. New York: Pantheon Books, 1971, p. 48.

3. Sir John Glubb, *The Life and Times of Muhammad*. Chelsea, MI: Scarborough House, 1970, p. 71.

4. Muhammad Husayn Hayka, *Muhammad*. London: Shorouk International, 1983, p. 63.

5. Rodinson, *Muhammad*, p. 51.

## Chapter 2: A Messenger for God

6. Ceasar E. Farah, *Islam: Beliefs and Observances*. Hauppauge, NY: Barrons Educational Series, 2000, p. 38.

7. Quoted in Rodinson, *Muhammad*, p. 43.

8. *Sura 96, The Noble Qur'an*, trans. Dr. Muhammad Taqi-ud-Din Al-Hilali and Dr. Muhammad Muhsin Khan. Madinah, K.S.A.: King Fahd Complex for the Printing of the Holy Qur'an, 2001, p. 842.

9. Muhammad Ibn Ishaq, *The Life of Muhammad*, trans. A. Guillaume. Karachi, Pakistan: Oxford University Press, 1997, p. 106.

10. *The Qur'an, Sura 94: 1–5*, p. 842.

11. Tor Andrae, *Muhammad: The Man and His Faith*, trans. Theophil Menzel. Freeport, NY: Books for Libraries Press, 1936, reprinted 1971, pp. 93–94.

12. Quoted in Rodinson, *Muhammad*, p. 74.

13. Quoted in Armstrong, *Muhammad*, p. 102.

14. Armstrong, *Muhammad*, p. 106.

## Chapter 3: The Early Muslims Meet with Opposition

15. Ishaq, *The Life of Muhammad*, p. 118.

16. Armstrong, *Muhammad*, p. 62.

17. *Qu'ran, Sura 73: 8–9*, p. 794

18. Karen Armstrong, *Jerusalem: One City, Three Faiths*. New York: Alfred A. Knopf, 1996, p. 224.

## Chapter 4: Hijra, The Flight to Yathrib (Medina)

19. Ishaq, *The Life of Muhammad*, p. 199.

20. *Sura 247*, quoted in Armstrong, *Muhammad*, p. 156.

21. Rodinson, *Muhammad*, p. 150.

22. Quoted in Martin Lings, *Muhammad: His Life Based on the Earliest Sources*. Rochester, NY: Inner Traditions International, 1983, p. 133.

23. Quoted in W. Montgomery Watt, *Muhammad: Prophet and Statesman*. London: Oxford University Press, 1961, p. 94.

24. Glubb, *The Life and Times of Muhammad*, p. 162.

25. Armstrong, *Muhammad*, p. 166.

## Chapter 5: Raids and Battles

26. Rodinson, *Muhammad*, p. 162.

27. Alfred Guillaume, *Islam*, quoted in Glubb, *The Life and Times of Muhammad*, p. 167.

28. Armstrong, *Muhammad*, p. 171.

29. Armstrong, *Muhammad*, p. 208.

## Chapter 6: The Return to Mecca

30. Glubb, *The Life and Times of Muhammad*, p. 269.

31. Armstrong, *Muhammad*, p. 220.

## Chapter 7: The Final Years

32. Lings, *Muhammad*, p. 286.

33. Glubb, *The Life and Times of Muhammad*, pp. 291–92.

34. Kitab al Maghazi, a chronicle of the Prophet's campaigns by Muhammad ibn 'Umar al Waqidi, ed. Marsden Jones, quoted in Lings, *Muhammad*, p. 298.

35. Rodinson, *Muhammad*, p. 262.

36. Quoted in Glubb, *The Life and Times of Muhammad*, p. 345.

37. Al-Bukhari, *Summarized Al-Bukhari*, trans. Dr. Muhammad Muksin Khan. Riyadh, Saudi Arabia: Maktaba Dar-as-Salam, 1994, pp. 882–83.

38. Quoted in James Michener, "Islam: The Misunderstood Religion," *Reader's Digest*, May 1955, p. 70.

39. Armstrong, *Muhammad*, p. 262.

# For Further Reading

## Books

Leila Azam and Aisha Gouverneur, *The Life of the Prophet Muhammad.* London: Islamic Text Society, 1985. Written from the Muslim point of view, this biography for young people includes many of the legends from the *Hadith.*

Matthew S. Gordon, *Islam: World Religions.* New York: Facts On File, 2001. A well-illustrated survey of Islam from its beginnings to the present day.

Shahrukh Husain, *Mecca.* New York: Dillon Press, 1993. Many color photos bring Saudi Arabia and its people alive. Customs, traditions, and history are combined to give the reader an insight into the holy city of Mecca.

Betty Kelen, *Muhammad: The Messenger of God.* Nashville: Thomas Nelson, 1975. A biography of Muhammad written in a narrative style.

Elsa Marston, *Muhammad of Mecca: Prophet of Islam.* New York: Franklin Watts, 2001. A young adult biography about the prophet's life and the message of Islam.

M.M. Pickthall, *The Life of the Prophet Muhammad: A Brief History.* Beltsville, MD: Amana, 1998. A concise look at the prophet's life and times from an Islamic point of view.

## Websites

www.islam101.com. An educational site that includes information about Muhammad as well as Islamic beliefs, way of life, culture, archaeology, art, history, and science.

www.muhammad.net. An interesting website with biographies about the prophet, quotes, and basic Islamic beliefs.

**Muslim History** (http://cyberistan.org). A short biography of the prophet Muhammad by Dr. A. Zahoor, author of *Muslim History, 570–1950 C.E.*, and Dr. Z. Haq.

**Muslim Student Association/University of Southern California** (www.usc.edu). An extensive collection about Muhammad's life and times, issues of Islam, and an extensive glossary.

**The Prophet Muhammad** (www.prophet muhammad.org). An Islamic website with easily accessed information on his biography, the cultural and historical setting of seventh-century Arabia, and controversies surrounding Muhammad's life.

**Saudi Arabia's American Website** (www. saudiembassy.net). Information about Saudi Arabia includes the Islamic calendar, easy-to-read map, *hajj* travel requirements, and up-to-date press releases about the Middle East.

**Saudi Arabia Information Resource** (www. saudinf.com). The official website for the Ministry of Information of Saudi Arabia includes extensive information about the country including maps, the history of Islam and Muhammad, and color photos of Medina and Mecca.

# Works Consulted

### Books

Al-Bukhari, *Summarized Al-Bukhari*. Trans. Dr. Muhammad Muksin Khan. Riyadh, Saudi Arabia: Maktaba Dar-as-Salam, 1994. This contemporary translation makes the work of the ninth-century Islamic historian accessible to young readers.

Tor Andrae, *Muhammad: The Man and His Faith*. Trans. Theophil Menzel. Freeport, NY: Books for Libraries Press, 1936, reprinted 1971. A thoughtful work, this book explores the spiritual message of Muhammad in the context of his life.

Karen Armstrong, *Jerusalem: One City, Three Faiths*. New York: Alfred A. Knopf, 1996. This well-written book has an interesting passage describing Muhammad's night journey to Jerusalem.

———, *Muhammad: A Biography of the Prophet*. San Francisco: Harper San Francisco, 1992. An understandable biography, this book makes use of ancient and contemporary sources to explore the importance of Muhammad's life in view of contemporary history.

R.V.C. Bodley, *The Messenger: The Life of Mohammed*. Garden City, NY: Doubleday, 1946. This simply written biography offers some interesting insights into the prophet's life and times.

Emory C. Bogle, *Islam: Origin and Belief*. Austin, TX: University of Texas Press, 1998. This book gives a chronology of Islam from its beginnings to the modern era.

Thomas Carlyle, *On Heroes, Hero Worship, and the Heroic in History*. Ed. Archibald MacMechan. New York: Ginn, 1901. The famous nineteenth-century English essayist includes Muhammad as one of the prototypes of the hero in history.

John L. Esposito, ed., *The Oxford History of Islam*. Oxford: Oxford University Press, 1999. A comprehensive history of Islam from its beginnings to the present.

Ceasar E. Farah, *Islam: Beliefs and Observances*. Hauppauge, NY: Barron's Educational Series, 2000. This book gives information about the contemporary practice of Islam.

Sir John Glubb, *The Life and Times of Muhammad*. Chelsea, MI: Scarborough House, 1970. A fascinating biography of Muhammad, this book provides the reader with notable dates and easy to follow lists of the many individuals who were important in Muhammad's life.

Muhammad Husayn Haykal, *The Life of Muhammad*. London: Shorouk International, 1983. Offers the reader many interesting details from the *Hadith* about Muhammad's life.

Philip K. Hitti, *History of the Arabs.* London: MacMillan, 1956. Provides information about the early history of the Arab people.

Muhammad Ibn Ishaq, *The Life of Muhammad.* Trans. A. Guillaume. Karachi, Pakistan: Oxford University Press, 1997. A readable translation of the work of the eighth-century Muslim scholar, this book contains many *hadiths* and is considered a primary source for scholars studying Muhammad's life.

Jacques Jomier, *How to Understand Islam.* New York: Crossroad, 1989. An explanatory book about the current practices of Islam.

Bernard Lewis, *The Arabs in History.* New York: Harper and Row, 1966. Looks at the history of the Arab people from ancient times to the present.

——, *Race and Slavery in the Middle East.* New York: Oxford University Press, 1990. A scholarly book about the history of race and slavery in the Arab world.

Martin Lings, *Muhammad: His Life Based on the Earliest Sources.* Rochester, NY: Inner Traditions International, 1983. This excellent source on the life of Muhammad is based on sources from the eighth and ninth centuries.

D.S. Margoliouth, *Mohammadanism.* London: Williams, 1925. This short survey of Muslim history contains an interesting chapter about the life of Muhammad.

*The Noble Qur'an in the English Language.* Trans. Dr. Muhammad Taqi-ud-Din Al-Hilali and Dr. Muhammad Muhsin Khan. Madinah, K.S.A.: King Fahd Complex for the Printing of the Holy Qur'an, 2001. This easily understood translation of the Qur'an is written in contemporary English.

Maxime Rodinson, *Muhammad.* Trans. Anne Carter. New York: Pantheon Books, 1971. An excellent source for learning about Muhammad's life, this book draws on early sources.

W. Montgomery Watt, *Muhammad: Prophet and Statesman.* London: Oxford University Press, 1961. A well-written biography of Muhammad that is accessible and easy to read.

——, *What Is Islam?* New York: Frederick A. Praeger, 1968. This book discusses the practices of contemporary Islam.

Ira O. Zepp Jr., *A Muslim Primer.* Fayetteville: University of Arkansas Press, 2000. An explanation of Islamic practices, including a brief but scholarly look at the life and times of Muhammad.

### Periodical

James Michener, "Islam: The Misunderstood Religion," *Reader's Digest*, May 1955.

# Index

'Abbas (uncle), 16, 32, 82
Abd Allah (Abdullah)
    (father), 15
Abd Allah (son), 23
Abdullah ibn Ubbayy, 56, 67,
    70–72
Abdul Muttalib (grandfather),
    14–15, 17–18, 39
Abraham, 58, 84
Abu al-Qasim. *See*
    Muhammad ibn Abd Allah
Abu Bakr (friend)
    becomes first Muslim
        caliph, 90, 94–95
    breaks up fight between the
        Quraysh and
        Muhammad, 41
    converts to Islam, 31–32
    emigrates to Yathrib, 50–52
    leads pilgrimage to Mecca,
        91
    meets Muhammad, 19
    Muhammad marries
        daughter of, 45–46, 54
    pilgrimage to Mecca by,
        82
    power of, threatened, 72
    support of Muhammad by,
        33
    tells Muslims about
        Muhammad's death, 93
Abu Jafar at-Tabari, 41
Abu Jahl, 44
Abu Lahab (uncle), 32, 46
Abul-Hakam, 41
Abu Sufyan, 62, 68–69, 76,
    80–81, 85–88
Abu Talib (uncle)
    death of, 46
    educates Muhammad, 18
    moves to another part of
        Mecca, 44
    Muhammad adopts son of,
        24, 90

refuses to convert to Islam,
    32, 46
rejects match between
    Muhammad and Umm
    Hani, 20–21
takes Muhammad on
    caravan trips, 22
threatened by Quraysh
    delegation, 39
Abyssinia, 41–42, 44
*see also* Ethiopia
Abyssinians, 27
Aden, 17, 39
affair of the lie, 70–72
Aisha (wife)
    ability of, to interpret
        Muhammad's
        revelations, 81
    accused of adultery, 70–72
    engagement to
        Muhammad, 45–46, 54
    marries Muhammad, 33, 52
    objects to Muhammad's
        new wives, 82
    recalls Muhammad's last
        moments of life, 93
    relationship with
        Muhammad, 89–90
    teases Sawdah, 66
Al Amin. *See* Muhammad ibn
    Abd Allah
al-Aqsa, 47
Ali (cousin)
    adopted by Muhammad,
        24, 90
    converts to Islam, 35
    involvement in raids by,
        62–63
    marries Fatimah, 65, 90
    Muhammad teaches
        prayers to, 31
    pilgrimage to Mecca by, 82
    revolt against, 81
    sons of, 91

Allah
    daughters of, 15, 38–39, 41
    Muhammad's revelations
        from, 25–31
    prayers to, 10, 33
    as primary god, 14–15, 30
Aminah (mother), 15–17
amulets, 57
Andrae, Tor, 28, 45
angels. *See* Gabriel
animals, treatment of, 84
*anni Hegirae*, 51
Arabia
    Jews lose political power in,
        81
    marriages in, 54, 79
    Muslims gain control of, 95
    pilgrimages in, 30
    raids in, 59–60
    Ramadan celebration in, 35
    treatment of animals in, 84
    tribes in, pledge allegiance
        to Muslims, 88
    warfare in, 65
Arafat, plain of, 95
archery, 18
Armstrong, Karen
    describes *tawwaf*, 30
    on development and
        significance of the Koran,
        57
    on the importance of
        Muhammad, 97
    on Islam dividing families,
        35
    on the Ka'aba as a place of
        worship, 40
    on massacre of Bani
        Qurayzah clan, 74
    on Muhammad as a
        statesman, 56–57
    on Muhammad's
        denouncement of
        Nakkah raid, 62–63

on Muhammad's final
  revelation, 47
on outcome of
  Muhammad's pilgrimage
  to Mecca, 79
on rules of marriage in the
  Koran, 79
Assembly, 17–18
astronomy, 42
Atik. *See* Abu Bakr
Aw tribe, 48

Badr, Battle of, 63–64
Bahira, 22
*banat al-Lah*, 37
Bangladesh, 10
Bani Qurayzah clan, 73–74
Bani Sa'd tribe, 16
battle of the ditch, 72–74
*bay'at al-ridwan*, 77
Bedouins, 16, 39, 85
Bible, 27, 42
Bilal, 41, 53
Bogle, Emory C., 89, 95
branding animals, 84
Buruq, 47
Byzantine Empire, 17, 84–85,
  91

caliph, 32–33, 44, 81, 91
camels, 51–52, 76–77, 84, 95
caravans, 16–18, 21–22, 24, 39,
  49, 59–63
Carlyle, Thomas, 49
China, 18
Christianity, 18–19, 27, 33, 42
City of the Prophet. *See*
  Medina
communal prayers, 33
Companions, 49, 54–56, 59–60
Conquest of Khaybar, 80–81
Constitution of Yathrib, 56–57

*dajjal*, 66
Daughters of God, 37
desert, 15–16, 39
*Dhu al-Hajja*, 95
dogs, 84

Dome of the Rock, 47
"Doubters, The," 70
dowry, 22, 69

Egypt, 18, 39, 84, 96
Ethiopia, 17
  *see also* Abyssinia

fabrics, 17
Farah, Ceasar E., 25
Fatimah (daughter), 24, 65, 91
First Pledge of al' Aqabah, 48
Five Pillars of Faith, 89

Gabriel, 26–27, 31, 35, 47
Gaza, 17, 39
Glubb, John
  on Abu Bakr's personality
    and reputation, 33
  on death of Zayd, 85
  on Muhammad's
    childhood, 18
  on Muhammad's interest in
    women, 79
  on Muhammad's revelation
    on the Jewish clans, 56
  on the Quraysh's abilities to
    make quick decisions, 77
  on warfare in Arabia, 65
goats, 18, 95
God. *See* Allah
grain, 17
Grand Mosque, 95
Guillaume, Alfred, 60

*hadith*, 11–13, 89, 93
Hafsah (wife), 65–66, 82
*hajj*, 14–15, 30, 82, 89, 92–93,
  95
Halimah (foster mother), 16
Hamzah (uncle), 16, 32, 41, 60,
  63, 68–69
harems, 82, 89–91
Hasan (grandson), 91
Hashim clan, 14, 18, 35, 44, 51
*Hegira*, 49
Hell, 31
Helpers, 49, 55–56, 60

"Hero as Prophet, The"
  (Carlyle), 49
*hijra*, 51, 57
Hind, 68, 80
holy war, 62
horses, 84
Hubal, 15, 30
Hudaybiyah, 76–80
*hums*, 19
Husayn (grandson), 91
"Hypocrites, The," 70

Ibn Ishaq, 18, 33, 85
Ibrahim (son), 90–91
*Id-ul-Fitr*, 35
idols, 14–15, 34, 41, 87
India, 18, 39
Indonesia, 10
Iraq, 96
Islam
  converts to
    'Abbas, 82
    Abu Bakr, 31–32
    Abul-Hakam, 41
    Ali, 90
    Khalid ibn al-Walid, 83
    pagans, 91–92
    Umar ibn al-Khattab,
      43–44
    wives of Muhammad, 79
    in Yathrib/Medina,
      48–49, 66
  definition of, 31
  effects of Judaism and
    Christianity on, 27
  Five Pillars of Faith, 89
  lesser pilgrimage of, 82
  popularity of, 10
  slavery and, 21
  *zakat*, 88
  *see also* Koran; Muslims
*Islam* (Farah), 25
*Islam: Origin and Belief* (Bogle),
  89, 95
ivory, 17

Jafar (cousin), 81, 85
Jerusalem, 33, 47, 58

Muhammad declared prophet of, 27–28

Muhammad defeats, in Mecca, 87

Muhammad's family as member of, 14–15

Muslims raid caravans of, 59–63

persecution of Muslims by, 33–36

plans to murder Muhammad, 51

prevents Muhammad from entering Mecca, 75–77

rejects invitation to Muhammad's wedding, 82

skeptical of Muhammad's teachings, 33–36

Qusayy, 39

raids, 59–63

Rajab, 47, 60–61

Ramadan, 25, 35, 51

Red Sea, 17

robbers, 17

Rodinson, Maxine, 23, 54, 59, 87

Roman Empire, 84

Ruqayyah (daughter), 24, 32, 41, 44, 64–65

Sabean kingdom, 42

sacrifices, 76, 78, 84, 95

Safa, 82

Safiyah, 80–82

*salat*, 33, 53, 89

Sanctuary, 75–76, 82

Satanic verses, 41–43

Saudi Arabia, 95

Sawdah (wife), 45, 52, 66

Second Pledge of al' Aqabah, 49, 60

*shahadah*, 89

*shayk*, 19

Sheba, 42

sheep, 18, 95

shrines, 14–15, 30, 37–38

silks, 17

*siyam*, 89

slavery, 21–22, 24, 32–33, 73

spices, 17

spies, 75

spirits, 15, 27

Sura of Victory, 78–79

*suras*, 30

Syria

attacks by Muslims on, 96

Battle of Mota in, 84–85

caravans traveling to and from, 17–19, 21, 39

Christianity in, 27

Jews settle in, 70

Tabuk, 91

Taif, 37, 46, 87

*tawwaf*, 30

*tazaqqa. See* Islam

Treaty of Hudaybiyah, 77–80

Ubaydah ibn al-Harith, 60, 63

Uhud, 67, 70

Umar ibn al-Khattab (friend), 43–44, 65, 82

Umm Ayman, 32

Umm Habiba (wife), 81–82, 87

Umm Hani, 20–21

Umm Kulthum (daughter), 24, 65, 91

Usmah (grandson), 32–33

Uthman (son-in-law), 41, 64–65

Uthman ibn Affan (son-in-law), 31–32, 76–77

al-Uzzah, 15, 38–39, 41

veils, 79

"Verses of Choice," 89

"Verses of the Curtain, The," 79

violence, 30

Waraka ibn Nawfal, 27–28

Watt, W. Montgomery, 27

weapons, 17

wine, 17

women

Muhammad's treatment of, 80, 89–90

rules of marriage for, 69

segregation of, in mosques, 53

sold into slavery, 73

wearing of veils by, 79

Yathrib

Abdullah dies in, 15

challenges for Companions in, 54–56

constitution of, 56–57

leader of, 56

location of, 48

Muhammad immigrates to, 48–54

Muhammad's first visit to, 16

Muhammad's marriages in, 53–54

shrines near, 37

tensions in, 48–49

*See also* Medina

"Year of Deputations, the," 91

Year of the Elephant, 14

Yemen, 17, 27, 91

*zakat*, 88–89

Zamzam, 15

Zayd ibn Muhammad (son)

adopted by Muhammad, 22, 24

involvement in Battle of Mota, 85

involvement in raids by, 62

learns Muhammad's teachings, 31

marries Umm Ayman, 32

Zaynab (daughter), 24, 80, 83–84

# Picture Credits

Cover: Ascent of the Prophet Muhammad to Heaven by Aqa Mirak/Bridgeman Art Library

© Art Archive/Harper Collins Publishers, 96

© Art Archive/Tokapi Museum, Istanbul/ Harper Collins Publishers, 15, 40, 46, 64, 66, 68, 86, 92, 94

© SEF/ Art Resource, Inc., 23, 32

© Archivo Iconografico,S.A./CORBIS, 29

© Bettmann/CORBIS, 20, 78

© Hulton-Deutsch Collection/CORBIS, 34

© Owen Franken/CORBIS, 12

© Getty Images, 43, 55, 61

© Mary Evans Picture Library, 17, 26, 50, 52, 63, 71, 72, 88

# About the Author

Marilyn Tower Oliver is the author of over 250 articles for adults and children, which have appeared in national and regional publications such as the *Los Angeles Times, Dolls, Doll World*, and *Valley Magazine*, where she is a contributing editor. She has also written six books for young adults including *Natural Crafts* and *Alcatraz Island in American History* and also produces and hosts a southern California cable television talk show about opera called *"Opera! Opera! Opera!"*

She is a distinguished graduate of Stanford University where she also received a master of arts degree in secondary education. She lives in Los Angeles with two poodles and a Siamese cat.